D1032176

MONHEGAN

INSCRIPTION DRAWN FROM PLASTER CAST MADE IN 1855
BY A. C. HAMLIN
It is placed on boulder diagonally as shown below

From Schoolcraft's *Information Respecting Indian Tribes*, vol. 6

MONHEGAN FIVE MILES AWAY

MONHEGAN, THE CRADLE OF NEW ENGLAND

BY

IDA SEDGWICK PROPER

PORTLAND, ME.
THE SOUTHWORTH PRESS
1930

TO FISHERMEN OF ALL TIMES
AND OF ALL COUNTRIES,
WHOSE COURAGE AND FAITH MADE DISCOVERY OF THE
NORTH AMERICAN CONTINENT POSSIBLE,
THIS HISTORY OF ONE OF THEIR SAFE HAVENS
IS DEDICATED

Second Printing, 1953

MANUFACTURED IN U.S.A.

CONTENTS

ILLUSTRATIONS

ILLUSTRATIONS

INTRODUCTION

MONHEGAN has always welcomed fishermen to her harbor. Her location and favorable natural advantages have been of great value to that vocation. She has seen all types of fishing craft, from the frail canoes of the Indians, the ox-hide of the Norse and Irish, to the gayly-colored sails of the Portuguese, Basque and Bretons. Sailing vessels of all types, climes and nations have dropped their anchors in her harbor to stop for a catch of cod, haddock, mackerel and lobsters. Most of the pioneers of New England came to gain prosperity and a living from fishing, while fish, from Monhegan, furnished food to several of their starving settlements. The Island's history begins with fishing, today fishing is the main source of income of her residents.

Fishing has always been an honorable vocation. All the Apostles of Christ were fishermen, and ever since fishermen have been found trustworthy, ingenious and courageous. The Fishmonger's Company of London is the oldest company in England, and has furnished over sixty Lord Mayors of that city. Venice and Amsterdam started as fishing villages and their wealth today continues to be increased by this industry.

John Selman and Nicholas Broughton, fishermen of Marblehead, were the first naval commanders appointed by Washington; while the fisherman, Commodore Tucker, captured more guns from the British than that famous patriot Paul Jones; Jefferson made the fishing industry a matter of extensive inquiry in 1791. Fishing continues to be a profitable, as well as a sporting profession, and staid Presidents of the United States have enjoyed this sport with the fishing fraternity. Some of the most beautiful sights of Europe are found in Brittany and the north of Spain where the fishing fleets anchor, and where the great fish markets gleam with the wonderfully-colored catches of those beautiful inhabitants of the deep sea. Monhegan, too, is a picturesque fishing village, and boats, stages and fish provide sketching material for artists.

The material for this survey of the history of the famous fishing island, Monhegan, has been gleaned from historical sources available in the United States.

"I have chosen commonly to set down things in the very words of the records, and originals and of the authors themselves, rather than in my own, without framing and dressing them into more modern language whereby the sense is sure to remain entire as the writers meant it; whereas by affecting too curiously to change and model words and sentences, I have observed the sense itself to be often marred and disguised." — Rev. Mr. Strype.

As nearly every event of historic importance that has occurred, in which Monhegan has figured, and many other facts concerning her, have been the occasion of heated disputes among historians and other authorities, your author has thought it wise to quote important authorities whose words cannot lightly be questioned. Another reason for this treatment is that there is a charm, a freshness, and a full old-time flavor about these chronicles that never could be duplicated by any modern writer. Still another reason, if these are not enough, lies in the fact that it would be necessary for a person who wished to read the original matter to camp out in some great library and spend weeks of time finding the numerous authorities quoted. This would be a difficult affair to arrange for people living in a remote place, such as Monhegan.

The search has extended through the official documents and collections of the various historical societies of Maine, Massachusetts, Newfoundland, New York, and Canada; through original and translations of the Norwegian, French, Spanish, and other foreign authorities, and into the ancient and modern histories, travels, biographies, compilations, and similar material. Diligent work has also been done amongst the old maps, and charts, and material on the discovery of North America. Grateful acknowledgment is made to all such authorities and sources of information.

Maine was the frontier of American colonization to the North, while Monhegan Island was the first and strongest outpost. Maine's territory was divided under different local governments, and your author has yet to find a complete, clear, and unbiased history of the early period of the whole state under these conditions and influences.

The religious conflict between the well-established Catholic Church and the onset of Protestantism in England was always a disturbing factor in the orderly development of Maine. This continued through the French and Indian Wars. Maine's pioneers, while not unduly religious, yet were mostly allied to the Church of England in feeling, while the people of Massachusetts were strongly Puritan, this difference in religious beliefs has added to the confusion. This section of Maine was for many years like a ball that was batted from New York to Massachusetts, and back and forth, through one form or another of government, until most of the citizens of the little Maine settlements did not know to which they should pay allegiance. Even the court records are to be found first here and then there, and sometimes in very unexpected places indeed. But the fault was in the times, and not from the actions of the people of Maine.

Some of the ministerial historians of Massachusetts and Maine, with determined and obstinate opinions, have not always been helpful in clarifying Monhegan's history. However, as the years go by, religious controversies grow less, and there is now, apparently, a recession of the bitter feelings that so long held sway. Old records are being unearthed and published, and new material is steadily becoming available through the antiquarian and historical societies and the modern and unbiased searchers after unvarnished truth.

Monhegan has probably suffered more than any other place from a few of these minister historians. Her glory has been snatched away to adorn the histories of other communities, but, in spite of all these attempts, she is so fundamentally incorporated in the beginnings of English enterprise in America that she has never suffered a total eclipse. Most of Monhegan's historians, and she has had many, have started off their histories by saying, or inferring, that her history started two hundred years before, or that its beginning lies beyond records, in the uncertain history of the discovery of America. It was on account of this vagueness that your author has made the extensive search through all the old legends and obscure and faulty records of ancient times, hoping to somewhat clarify this portion of her history. The readers must judge for themselves of the results.

It has been only through the cordial coöperation of librarians that any result has been obtained. Thanks are due to Mr. Paulsits, chief, Mr. Taylor, librarian, and the staff, of the American History Section of the New York Public Library, Mrs. Marion Cobb Fuller, research librarian of the Maine State Library, Miss Hall, librarian of the Maine Historical Society

Library, and many, many other helpful people in the libraries of Boston and New York. Various friends have been of great service through their encouragement and enthusiasm, which has made the task less burdensome. Mistakes will undoubtedly be found, as errors will creep in where the ground covered is so extensive, so obscure, and where so many authorities have been dealt with. The author hopes that these errors will be few and of minor importance and will not greatly detract from the result.

Monhegan, Maine,
April 15, 1930.

[illegible]

thors, and many, many other helpful people in the libraries of Boston and New York. Various friends have been of great service through their encouragement and enthusiasm, which has made the task less burdensome. Mistakes will undoubtedly be found, as errors will creep in where the ground covered is so vast, the sources so uncertain, and where so many authorities have been dealt with. The author hopes that these errors will be few and of minor importance and will not greatly detract from the result.

[illegible]

[illegible]

MONHEGAN

"We sailed the next morning, bound east, and on our starboard side, as we neared the point, a lofty island, some four leagues away attracted our attention — it was Monhegan. When we returned from our exploration of the islands of the Penobscot and Mount Desert, we sighted the island, the morning sun playing on its top, bathed it in light; amid a peaceful ocean it rose like an island of the blessed; anon the lighthouse and then as with flowing sail we neared it, houses and then windows could be made out.

"The wind was fair, but on my suggestion that this was hallowed ground, the germ of New England, we hauled up a little closer to the wind and dashed up to the head of the harbor, tacked and stood off on our course, westward, ho! We had seen the cradle of New England."

HON. CHARLES LEVI WOODBURY, in *Pemaquid and Monhegan.*

CHAPTER I

DEEP sea islands have always had a vivid charm, a romantic fascination for mankind: Bards, chroniclers, dreamers, and poets have sung their pleasurableness in every language and they are deeply imbedded in the legends of ancient races. Fantastic tales of islands colored the records of all early voyages to the new world, and they even decorate the tales of Elizabeth's adventurous sea captains in search of a short route to the Spice Islands; today they still stir the imagination.

Monhegan is the most famous deep sea island on the Atlantic seaboard. Her place in the recorded history of the discovery of the American continent is still shrouded in fogs, just as her rocky heads are so often obscured by the wisps and wreaths of the circling fogs that haunt her shores. This obscurity is due to the secrecy imperative during that momentous period. But as the new records are dug up in old-world musty libraries, we glimpse her unmistakable outline, here and there, and the glorious place she held in the colonization of America.

In any consideration of Monhegan's history regard for her location in the deep sea, at the forefront of Maine's many islands, midway between the entrances to the Kennebec and Penobscot, and her many natural advantages, must be constantly kept in mind.

MONHEGAN

Monhegan is a great landmark, more remarkably so she must have been when primeval forests crowned her lofty heads, making her visible for a very great distance at sea. Isolated in deep water, "eight leagues from the main," every craft beating up or down the coast of the unknown continent was forced to observe her. It is but natural then that mention is so often made of "an island in 43½ of northerly latitude" in the scanty records that remain. She bore many names — some queer and very often obscure.

Her small size, too, was then an asset. Great hoards of hostile natives could not hide on such a comparatively small island surrounded by seas too rough to tempt their frail canoes. The snug, deep harbor, sheltered on three sides from the winds, with Manana concealing movements of vessels from hostile eyes on the mainland; sandy beaches, fit for landing small boats loaded with fish, were advantages not lost sight of by the adventurers.

Weary, storm-tossed mariners must many times have given thanks to their God, or gods, for her safe harbor, her wood for fuel, and her fresh spring water, as well as the delectable berries found everywhere in such abundance. That she was a haven beyond compare in an unknown, uncharted region is told by many thankful voyagers.

It has been thought necessary to go back to the old and legendary sources for tales of voyagers to this locality in order to account for the oldest vestige or possible sign of the occupation of, or landing on, Monhegan by such persons as might have chiseled the peculiar Inscription that is on Manana, Monhegan's little companion island.

This Inscription appears, and has always appeared, to be the work of man's hand, although several authorities have disputed it. It is placed on a boulder, in a diagonal manner, at right angles to the grain of the granite, or extremely hard volcanic rock, on which it is found. A drawing of it is shown in the frontispiece of this volume, which was made from a plaster cast taken in 1855, or seventy-five years ago. A comparison of the drawing with the original will show that there has been slight change due to weathering. If the Inscription is the work of nature, surely in seventy-five years nature would have continued her work and cracks would have appeared at each end of each supposed character, which would have entirely changed its appearance. This is not the case.

The Inscription alone might be passed over, by unbelievers, were it not for the large spring found near the base of the rock, on which the Inscription is graven, and from which the Inscription runs to the strange holes found on top of the rock or ledge above. These holes might have been made to fit rounded ends of poles or timbers, used to hold upright some structure to carry a cross, or other symbol of possession, or a signal, either of distress, or to attract the attention of passing craft to the fine spring, or good harbor, or both. These holes or depressions are arranged · :· so that the end one was evidently used as a brace. Placed in this location on Manana such a signal could not have been overlooked by any passing craft.

This Inscription has come in for endless discussions and many of the Massachusetts people have made merry over it along with their Dighton Rock. But that many people have held, and many others do now hold, the opinion that the Inscription is a very real one, although of unknown origin, is also a fact. It was first brought to notice in 1808, but the turmoil about it being of Norse origin did not begin until 1849; this continued at a furious rate until 1885, when someone with a magnifying glass found some faint cracks and discredited it. Due to these discussions the drawing was made, which now makes possible the comparison after such a long period by any reader. A résumé of the discussion for and against will be found in its chronological order. There was also another supposed inscription of similar characters on one of the ledges of the Peninsula of St. George which has been lost through vandalism. These are the only two such freaks of nature, if nature's work they are, that have been found in Maine up to date.

Partly on account of this still undeciphered Inscription on Manana, and also because Monhegan's history starts in mists and legends, consideration of ancient tales of islands in this general locality will be sketchily touched upon in this study.

If, as some of the earlier Maine historians hesitatingly suggest, the Inscription on Manana is not Norse, but still might be of Phoenician origin, some gleanings of the activities of this ancient people may be pertinent.

Cádiz, Spain (or Gades the ancient name), was the chief city of the region called Tarshish in the Bible and Tartessus in classical days. Its population in the earliest times came from Phoenicia, an ancient section of Greece, lying between Tesselia and Boeotia.

Cádiz became prominent about the year 1100 B.C. It lies further to the west than any other of the cities of Andalusia, or southern Spain, and was a famous maritime city. It was occupied by the Carthaginians in 501 B.C.—Carthage was also a Phoenician city—who had been summoned to the aid of the Gaditanians. The art of writing, the first and most important aid to commerce, was propagated from Gades. After the Second Punic War came the dominations of the Romans, who ultimately (27 A.D.) formed the whole of the south of Spain into the *Provincia Baetica.* Hamilcar, Hannibal and the Scipios fitted out their fleets in the Cádiz harbor.

The fish and preserved meats of Cádiz were celebrated in the second century after Christ. "In the middle of the 12th century, after a long period of Mahometan rule, Cádiz was important enough to make Edrisi greatly exaggerate on his map the size of its peninsula, making it an island, and giving it a name when most other islands went nameless."[1] "Pilotage and Hydrography" were taught in

[1] DeCosta.

Andalusia at a very early period, especially by Bascayan mariners. An ordinance from Ferdinand and Isabella, dated March 18, 1500, confirms the regulations which until then had been followed in a school of Basque pilots at Cádiz. The document declares the origin of the school so ancient that "the memory of man runneth not to the contrary (*que de tanto tiempo ace' que memoria de hombres non es en contario*)." The most celebrated pilot and cartographer of the time was a Basque, Juan de la Cosa, who accompanied Christopher Columbus on his first and second voyages, and whose map made in 1500 is the most important of that period.

Cádiz was destroyed during the middle ages and its revival dates with the discovery of America and the anchoring of the "silver fleet" in its harbor.

This seeming detour to Cádiz is given for the reason that on very old maps the words "Boethik," and "Boethem," are found placed on the regions in the northeast portions of North America, and since evidences of the occupation of the country by the Norsemen has not been substantiated by remains, the hue and cry is now turned toward the records of the "Boethiks." The Phoenicians were neighbors of the Boeotians.

The Phoenicians were great navigators, whose exploits remained unequaled till the days of Columbus. Hakluyt tells of their trips around Africa. The Phoenician sailors were in great demand to man the ships of all countries. Sails on Phoenician crafts were so arranged that they could sail only with the wind nearly aft. The prevailing winds at Cádiz are southwest during the winter months and as Cádiz is 36° N. L. and Monhegan 43° 45′ and 52″, these winds if continual could easily have brought them to this island. Cádiz has also the high tides like those that rise and fall on Monhegan's rocky shore.

From pure conjecture we now arrive at legends, about islands and voyages to this region.

Brendan,[2] an Irish monk, around 565 A.D., so the legend runs, heard of the existence to the west, in the ocean, of an Isle of Saints. He was immediately seized with a holy impulse to visit it. He embarked with seventeen followers of the brotherhood in an osier boat which was covered with tanned hides, well greased.

They reached, after about forty days, an island with steep scarped sides, where they were hospitably received and where they reprovisioned. Carried by the strong winds from the region of this island they came to an island where there were countless flocks of sheep. They took a lamb, so the story runs, and went to a barren island close by to celebrate Easter. When they landed they set up their altar, then made a fire intending to roast the lamb. To their consternation the island began to move. They fled to their boat and then found that they had been on the back of a whale ("Jasconius is his name") instead of on an island. They hastily got away and the next day they came to an island which only birds inhabited. They re-

[2] From story in Stokes, *Iconographie of Manhattan Island.*

mained on this island until Pentecost, then wandered for several months on the ocean. At last they came to the island of which St. Patrick was the patron saint. Here they celebrated Christmas, again embarking after the octave of the Epiphany. They passed a year in these travels, al-

ST. BRENDAN'S WHALE
From Stokes *Iconographie of Manhattan Island*

ways peering out for the Isle of Saints. For six years they visited and roamed between these various islands, but during the seventh year they found to the north a rocky, barren island of Cyclop's forges; this they thought the mouth of hell. Finally they found themselves in a region of mist and darkness, and discovered the long sought Isle of Saints. They remained here for forty days, and then an angel appeared and told them to return to their own country.

This is the story as it has come down, but that some belief in its verity existed in the minds of cartographers seems certain, for St. Brendan's Island is placed on the ancient maps at the forefront of the unexplored regions, and as *Terre Nuova* was being talked about they shifted its position hither and yon in the ocean until it found an anchorage on the charts near the uncertain outlines of the Gulf of Maine and on one ancient map it occupies a position nearly that of Monhegan.

But St. Brendan was not the only Irish voyager to turn his craft westward. Early in the Christian era the Irish, a restless, an energetic, a hardy seafaring folk, became Christian zealots and their missionaries went through Europe trying to convert the world. The English and Scots resented them. Finally schism in the church brought about their persecution and they fled in their half-decked, ox-hide vessels of the period to the islands of the far North Atlantic.

From here they were driven by the Norsemen, their bitter foes, to the Faröe Islands. Their enemies reached them there and they pushed to sea, until they found a new home in Iceland. These migrations were during a period from the sixth to the ninth century.

The Irish historian Dieuil and the Icelandic Landnamabok, or book of land acquisitions, relate that when the Norse first reached Iceland they found living there a Christian people called the Papas — or Culdees of Ireland.

Again their Norse foes drove them out and they had nowhere to go, so they embarked in their boats, commended themselves to God, and sailed to the west.

In this direction they found a new land, which, on account of its size, they called Irland it Mikla, or Ireland the Great. From this time they endeavored to hide their place of refuge, but the Northmen hung on to their trail and it is from the sagas that we learn of their settlement in the new world.

Are' Thorgelsson, surnamed Frodhe' or the Wise (Gaffarel), who lived from 1067 to 1148, left an account which was completed by five other historians. Here is what he says of his great-grandfather, Are' Marsson.

"Are' son of Ma'r and Torkatla, was driven by a storm to Hvitramannaland (or Whiteman's land, or land of men in white), which some call Ireland it Mikla. This country is situated westward in the sea, near Vineland the Good, it is said at 6 days sail from Ireland."

An old manuscript,[3] quoted by Rafn in *Antiquitates Americanae,* is fairly explicit as to locality.

"Now there are, as is said, south from Greenland, which is inhabited, deserts, uninhabited places and icebergs, then the Skrellings, then Markland, then Vineland the Good. Next, and farther behind lies Albania, which is white man's land. Thither was sailing formerly from Ireland, there Irishmen and Icelanders recognized Ari, the son of Mar and Kalta of Reykjaness, of whom nothing

[3] Codex 770 of the Arne Magneau collection.

has been heard for a long time and who had been made a chief there by the inhabitants."

Eric the Red's Saga and the Saga of Thorfinn Karlsefni tell of native boys captured in Markland, an American region, about 1006, who told of a country beyond their own, where people wore white garments and carried rags on poles and shouted; from which it was inferred that this must be, as already known or rumored, "White Man's Land," sometimes called Great Ireland.

From an ancient volume:

"We finde in the old manuscript life of S. Brendan that many of them (Irish) were sent into, and lived in the Iles of America and had been there, some 80 years, some 90; brought up by St. Patrick, in his monasteries in these parts before."[4]

There are also records of a Welsh settlement in this western country of the Atlantic and this is what B. F. DeCosta prints in confirmation of this fact:

"Pre-Columbian Geneologies compiled by Ilvan Brecoa say that 'Madoc and Riryd found land far in the west and settled there.' Madoc, son of Gwynedd, Prince of Wales, a sailor, adventurous on the sea, made a voyage westward on the Atlantic, after the first voyage he was supposed to have been murdered, while, on trial, the accused man was cleared. He reappeared in Wales, raised

[4] Manuscript, Antiq. Capgrave tin S. Brendan. Menmius Histor. sup. Mueth Westm. Anno 491, Antiq. Glastonien Capgrave in S. Piran, published by Richards Boughton in 1655.

a company of 300 men and women, embarked in 10 ships with the intention of returning to the site of his colony. He sailed westward for the purpose of founding a colony and never returned."

Hakluyt uses the Madock legend as an argument for the possession of the new country by Queen Elizabeth, as did Dee and other of her councilors. Hakluyt says:

"And it is very evident that the planting there shall in time amply enlarge her Majesties Territories and Domenions, or (I might rather say) restore to her Highness ancient right and interest in those countries into the which a noble and royall personage, lineally descended from the blood royall, borne in Wales, names Madock ap Owen Gwyneth, departing from the coast of England, about the yeere of our Lord God 1170, arrived and there planted himselfe and his colonies and afterward returned himselfe into England, leaving certaine of his people there, as appeareth in an ancient Welsh Chronicle, where he then gave to certaine Ilands, beasts and foules sundry Welsh names, as the Iland of Penquin, which yet to this day beareth the same."

CHAPTER II

THE Northmen in the eighth and ninth centuries were renowned sailors; hardy, adventurous, and furious warriors. They sailed, in their large skin-covered boats, into the rivers of Russia and France, conquering as they went. Rollen, one of their chiefs, obtained Normandy, a part of France, which was then settled by Norsemen and which has always retained traces of them. They roamed as far as the Mediterranean and even reached Constantinople; they disturbed the last days of Charlemagne and finally one of them, William the Conqueror, a Duke of Normandy, invaded and conquered England in 1066.

Being such restless, virile mariners, it is not at all strange or remarkable that they should have wandered to the coasts of North America, to Markland and Vinland the Good, and the tales of such voyages as related in the sagas gain weight in face of their heroic exploits during this period.

It would seem unnecessary to relate the voyages of the Norsemen in a brief history of Monhegan were it not for the fact that in reaching Vinland the Good they had to sail by, and perhaps may even have landed in the Monhegan harbor on one of their numerous voyages to this wonderful land. These expeditions continued during several hundreds of years and it would seem very improbable, indeed, that they should fail to notice Monhegan when, through the testimony of the later voyagers, Spanish, Portuguese, French and English, she was such a prominent landmark and had such a convenient harbor away out in the deep sea. It is probable that Markland or Vinland the Good was the country later called Drogeo by the Zeni brothers and still later Norumbega (or the country of the Norsemen), by the seekers after a short passage to Cathay or the Northwest Passage. Norumbega is the old Spanish word meaning Norwegian or Northmen.

We also have in mind the quest of the historians for the interpretation of the supposed Norse Inscription on Manana which commenced in 1845 or thereabouts and continued for many years. This will be noticed in its chronological order.

Naddod, a Scandinavian, in 860 A.D., and Gardar, a Dane, driven by storms, sighted and explored Iceland; Ingolf in 874 settled there. He found the Christian Irishmen, or the "Papas," already there and drove them out. Later Eric the Red, in 986, driven from Iceland founded a settlement in Greenland.

In 990 Biarne, storm driven out of his course between Greenland and Iceland, saw a strange land, consisting of three distinct countries evidently some part of New England, then Nova Scotia and last Newfoundland. Biarne told of his discoveries in Iceland and this news was wafted by the Norseman's sail to Norway. Biarne received considerable censure for not having explored the new country.

Leif, son of Eric the Red, undertook to find out about this strange land in 1000. He bought Biarne's ship, took Biarne and thirty-five men along with him and came first to the country that Biarne had seen last. Leif named it after its nature, "Helluland" or stone land. They pursued their voyage and found Biarne's second and wood-covered land. This Leif named "Markland" or woodland. Continuing their course they found a very pleasant country which Leif named Vinland, because they found vines or wineberries there. Dr. Fernald states that these vines might have been cranberry vines. They also found wheat, "self sown," bears, and various kinds of woods. They spent the winter in this pleasant country, filling their vessel with wood and returned to Iceland in the spring.

After this voyage Vinland became the subject of talk and conjecture among the mariners and led to a voyage undertaken by Leif's brother, Thorwald, for further exploration. Thorwald borrowed Leif's ship, took some of the men who had accompanied Leif for pilots and accomplished the voyage to Leif's former camp or Leifsbudir, as they called it, in 1002. Here they spent the winter fishing and cutting wood and in the spring of 1003 Thorwald sent a party in the ship's longboat on a reconnaissance expedition to the south without much success. The party spent the winter of 1003 in Leifsbudir and in the spring of 1004 Thorwald, himself, undertook another voyage of exploration from Leifsbudir eastward and then to the north, "around the country." On this expedition he damaged the keel of his ship and so landed on a promontory, where he remained some time repairing it. He named this high promontory "Kialarnes," meaning ship-nose, and then sailed to the mainland. This promontory, being like a ship's nose, might possibly have been Monhegan as Champlain in 1604 called the island La Nef or Ship Island. As far as this study has gone no other promontory in this vicinity has been named by early voyagers from its resemblance to a ship.

Thorwald came to anchor on the mainland not far from a hilly promontory overgrown with wood and was so pleased with the place that he exclaimed, "Here it is beautiful, and here I should like to fix my abode." A little later the voyagers had an encounter with the natives and Thorwald was mortally wounded with an arrow. He instructed his men to bury him on his beautiful promontory and to place two crosses, one at his head, the other at his feet, and to call the place "Krossanaes," the promontory of the crosses.

Thorwald's men returned to their companions at Leifsbudir and spent the winter of 1004 there. In the spring of 1005, with the cargo of wood, furs and grapes, probably dried, they returned to Greenland with the news of Thorwald's death.

Thorstein, Eric's third son, then decided to go to Vinland to recover the body of his brother. He fitted out the same ship and with his wife Gudrida and twenty-five men set forth. The ship was storm-driven the whole summer and when they finally returned to Greenland, Thorstein sickened and died.

In the summer of 1006, Thorfinn Karlsefni, a wealthy Icelander, arrived in Greenland, fell in love with Gudrida, Thorstein's widow, and married her during the winter. Thorfinn, probably urged by Gudrida who wanted to see Vinland, prepared three ships in the summer of 1007. One ship was commanded by himself, another by Biarne, accompanied by Thorhall the hunter, and the third by Thorwald who had married Freydisa, a natural daughter of Eric the Red. They had a company of one hundred and sixty, and the purpose of the voyage was one of colonization, as they took live stock with them.

Sailing from Greenland in a southerly course, in the spring of 1008, they came to "Helluland," and from thence two days in a southerly direction to "Markland," considered by many historians as Nova Scotia, by others Maine. From here they coasted "to the south-west, having land always on their starboard," finally arriving at "Kialarnes," or ship's nose. Continuing their voyage they came to "long sandy beaches and downs," which they called "Furdustrandr," or wonderstrand.

One version of the story relates that Thorhall the hunter wished to explore northward of wonderstrand, or "Vinland," while Thorfinn Karlsefni desired to proceed southward. At any rate Thorhall went to an island to prepare for his trip taking nine men with him. There is a song supposed to have been sung by Thorhall while on this island, which has been interpreted as follows:

> When I came, these brave men told me,
> Here the best of drink, I'd get,
> Now with water-pail behold me, —
> Wine and I are strangers yet.
> Stooping at the Spring, I've tested
> All the wine this land affords;
> Of its vaunted charms divested,
> Poor indeed are its rewards.

Evidently Thorhall did not find the wine he craved. Thorhall sailed along "Furdustrandr" and "Kialarnes," and then encountered a wild northwest storm which drove his ship into the ocean. He was finally reported as having reached the shores of Ireland, and according to the accounts of some merchants, he and his men were enslaved by the Irish, the implacable foes of the Norse.

Thorfinn Karlsefni with his company stayed for three years at their settlement. During this time a son, called Snorre, was born to him.

Thorfinn in 1009 made a searching expedition for Thorhall. He sailed to the north to "Kialarnes" and then to the west, "having the country on his left side." He came to anchor in the mouth of a river where he saw what they called a "Onefoot" or a "Uniped," who, being hidden behind some trees, killed with an arrow one of Thorfinn's men. After this unhappy affair, Thorfinn continued his search northward. Finding no trace of his man Thorhall, and fearful of the country of the "Onefoots" he returned to the south. The onefoot was probably the seal and the arrow shot by an Indian concealed nearby. At any rate Maine was probably known for a time to the Norse as the "Country of the Onefoots."

In 1011 Karlsefni and his family returned to Greenland, probably leaving some of the company behind, and carrying away two native youths of Markland as captives; their ships richly laden with the products of the country.

Two brothers, Helge and Finnboge, arrived in Greenland from Norway just at the time of Thorfinn Karlsefni's return, and excited by the rich rewards of this expedition to Vinland, arranged with Freydisa, the wife of Thorwald, for an expedition. Freydisa knew and liked Vinland the Good and wanted to enrich herself with the country's products so she made a business arrangement with them, and sailed with these two brothers and a company in 1012. A disagreement occurred between Freydisa and the brothers and they were slain. She then returned, with her companions, to Greenland where the rich cargo of Thorfinn Karlsefni was still being loaded. She probably sold a part at least of her spoils to him as he sailed for Norway with the richest cargo that had ever left Greenland up to that time.

These are, exceedingly briefly told, the recorded voyages of the Norse to Vinland the Good. The tales are to be found principally in three books: The Friis Book, of 1260; Hauk's Book, of 1299-1334; The Flatey (Island) Book, a century later. They are records called sagas, made from word of mouth tales handed down from one generation to another and served mainly as land acquisition records.

Gudrida, after the death of Thorfinn Karlsefni and the marriage of Snorre, made a pious pilgrimage to Rome, where she told some of the Pope's household about Vinland the Good and the settlements made there.

Afterwards, as the Vatican records show, a Bishop was sent to Vinland and there are also records of Peter's Pence being collected from the settlers there. These Vatican records, rather recently unearthed, would corroborate the conjecture of Ortelius, that Norumbega was a settlement of Norsemen, almost forgotten.

We have also the testimony of Adam of Bremen, who wrote an *Ecclestical History of the North of Europe*[5] in 1073, that the King of Denmark, Sueno, to whom he paid a visit, mentioned to him a country.

". . . one which they call Vinland, because the vine would grow there without cultivation, and because it produced the best sort of wine. That besides, plenty of fruits grow in this country without planting, is not mere opinion, but I have this news from very authentic and trustworthy relations of the Danes."

Another historian, Ordericus Vitalis, born in England, and afterwards Bishop of Rouen in Normandy, appears to have known something about Vinland, and to have

[5] Adam of Bremen, *Descripto insularum Aguilonis Gesta Hammabugenis, 1069-1076; Ecclesiae pontificum, 1595.*

mentioned it in his *Ecclestical History*, written one hundred years after Thorfinn's expedition.

Thus it appears that Vinland was a well-known and a very definite place during the middle ages.

After this voyage of colonization to Vinland no special voyages are recorded in detail in the sagas. Travel back and forth was probably an ordinary occurrence and no more mention is made of these parts. We find, however, two more voyages noted to the westward. One was that of a bishop, named Erik, who went to Vinland in 1121 on a missionary expedition. This would probably indicate that a colony of some size was located there, as usually bishops are not sent to small communities.

In 1285 two clergymen, Aldahzand and Thorwald Helgason, visited on the west coast of Iceland a new land. Some years after this voyage the King of Denmark, Erik the Priest-hater, sent out a ship under the command of Rolf, to pay a visit to this new land. But nothing has been noted concerning its results.

Again, about one hundred years after this event, we find, in the ancient Icelandic Annals, the following remarkable, though short report:

"In the year 1347 a vessel, having a crew of seventeen men, sailed from Iceland to Markland." The dry and brief manner in which this is reported seems to prove that this vessel of 1347 was not driven to "Markland" by chance or storms, but that the expedition was intentional, undertaken probably for the purpose of getting timber and other supplies from that country. The accident of this vessel losing her anchors through a storm seems to account for the item being recorded.

The Icelandic Annals, however, as Professor Rafn has cited, show that voyages were made from time to time down to the middle of the fourteenth century from Iceland and Greenland to the continent to the south for timber, for fishing or for carrying the Christian religion to the natives. They left no permanent remains of dwellings for, as the sagas relate, these were constructed of timber that would either be burned by the Indians or suffered a natural decay before the landing of the English.

In the search for records concerning Pre-Columbian voyages to North America, the sagas have been translated many times by students, with variations as to the meaning of important words, what the Norse meant when they spoke of the length of night and day, their calculations of sailing time, distance, climate, products, and numerous other matters.

Each translation has been interpreted differently by the different writers, English, Norse, French, and American — in fact the whole subject of Norse voyages to Vinland the Good is a seething whirlpool of conjecture, surmise and determined opinion by localizing historians. The whole body of Norse-discovery literature has, therefore, become so distasteful to many historians that they are tempted to go to the other extreme and throw the whole of these legendary tales overboard.

CHAPTER III

THESE vague tales bring us down to the time of the Zeni brothers. Around the close of the fourteenth century, or about 1380, Nicolo Zeno, wealthy and noble Venetian, fitted out a ship for a voyage to England. Driven by storms further north, he finally arrived at a group of islands called by him "Friesland" and now known to us as the Faröe Islands. These islands had been in the possession of the Northmen since 861.

The Norman, or ruling lord, Zichmni, having revolted against the King of Norway, welcomed Zeno and his ship, and made him prime minister and chief admiral. Nicolo Zeno then invited his brother Antonio, who was living in Venice, to join him in this hospitable group of islands. This invitation Antonio accepted, arriving there in the year 1391. They made voyages and explorations in every direction until 1395 when Nicolo died.

Antonio Zeno continued to live in the north and was so interested in the discoveries and adventures of his brother and himself in these little-known countries, that he wrote, or finished writing, a report concerning them and on a sea chart depicted all the surrounding countries of which he or his brother had knowledge. This was probably considerably augmented by knowledge supplied by fishermen and other Northmen. This volume Antonio sent to a third brother, Carlo Zeno, at Venice. Antonio died in the north in 1404, so the volume must have reached Venice between the years 1395 and 1404.

Carlo Zeno put this valuable contribution to the little-known regions of the north in his archives, as a memorial of his brothers, where it remained undisturbed for one hundred and fifty years. During these one hundred and fifty years the volume decayed and became very greatly damaged. In 1558, after the art of printing came into use, Nicolo Zeno, the younger, rescued what remained of the volume and the chart and had it printed.

It is interesting to note that many of the early discoverers of America were Italians: Notably Columbus, Cabot and Verrazano. Cabot was a Venetian and the Zeni material may have reached his hands.

Antonio Zeno, in the report on his and his brother's voyages, relates that a fishing vessel from "Frisland," being driven by a storm far out to the west, arrived at a country named "Estotiland," the inhabitants of which had commerce with "Engroenelandt" (Greenland). This country, "Estotiland," was very fertile, and had mountains in the interior. The king of the country had in his possession some books written in Latin, which, however, he did not understand. The language which he and his subjects spoke had no similarity to the Norse.

The King of Estotiland, seeing that his guests sailed in much safety with the assistance of an instrument (the compass), persuaded them to make a maritime expedition to another country to the south called "Drogeo" or "Droceo." There they had the misfortune to fall into the hands of a most barbarous tribe, and they were all killed except one, who was made a slave, but who after a long time, and with many adventures, found his way back to Greenland and to the Faröe. He related that the country Drogeo stretched far to the south, and was a very large country, like another world, and it was full of savage tribes, who covered themselves with skins and lived by hunting. They had no other weapons than bows and arrows and lived among each other in an eternal warfare. But far off to the south were some more civilized nations which knew the use of the previous metals, and built towns and temples; it was, however, their custom to kill their prisoners and offer them to their gods. This was probably the accumulated knowledge of many voyages and adventures instead of the one lone captive.[6] These more "civilized nations" may well have been those dwellers in Central America, whose temples and villages Lindbergh has been flying over and exploring during the past year.

On this map we are only interested in the countries "Estotiland" and "Drogeo" or "Droceo." The word "Estotiland" has excited the historians for several centuries, and so far has not been explained satisfactorily. Many have made conjectures as to the meaning of the name. The Frenchman Beauvois wrote a monograph attempting to

[6] Kohl, *Me. Hist. Soc. Coll. Doc. Hist.*, vol. 1, pp. 104-5.

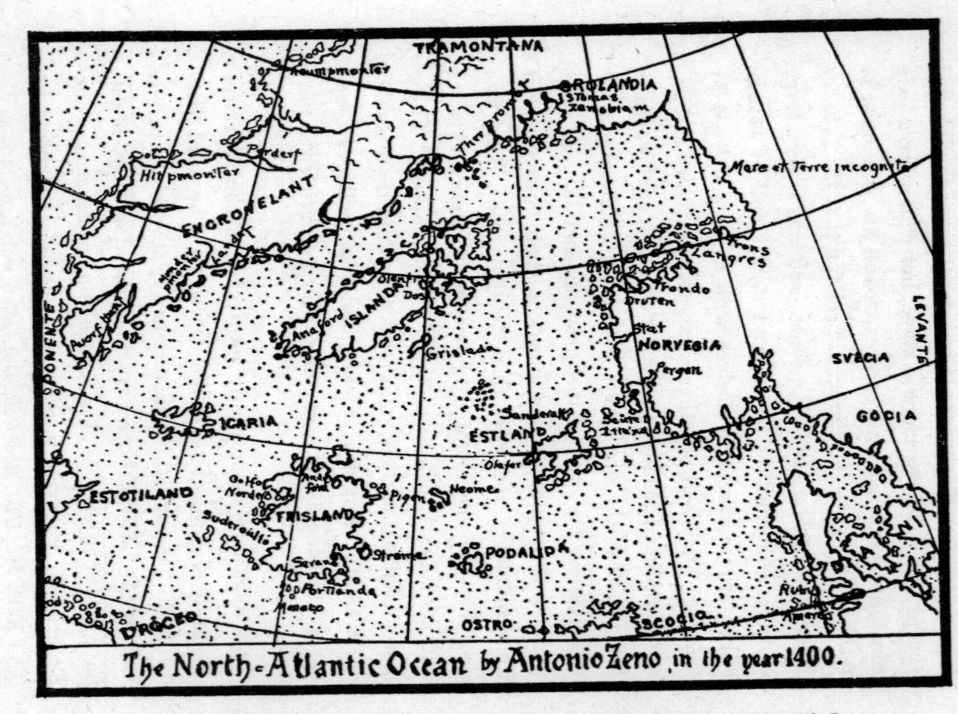

From Kohl, "Discovery of Maine." *Me. Hist. Soc. Coll. Doc. Hist.*, vol. I

explain "Estotiland" as a country inhabited by the Scots. He naïvely changed the t's to c's and called it "Escociland," or land of the Scots. Dr. Kohl has found a German meaning for it, translating it to "East Outland."

If old dictionaries were available we would probably find that "Estotiland" was named as Eric is said to have named "Helluland," "Markland" and "Vinland," after the kind of commodities found there. Probably we should also be able to prove that "Estotiland" was a common or fisherman's term applied to stockfish grounds which was later called "baccalao." In a Spanish dictionary today there is a commercial name for stockfish, which is not dissimilar, in estocafis. Another explanation might be that the word had some connection with the manner of harpooning whales. Estoc is an ancient French term for a rapier.

"Drogeo" or "Droceo," is, according to Dr. Kohl, probably New England. Certainly it has the numerous islands which have always distinguished the coast of Maine on ancient maps. This name seems to have escaped the recorded surmises of the historians. It, too, like Estotiland probably received its name because of its rare commodities—drugs—which later voyagers sought for and found in this locality.

Abraham Ortelius evidently believed the Zeni account for in *Theatrum Orbis,* fol. 6, he says:

"And here I shall not commit any great inconvenience, or absurdities, in adding unto this History of the New

World, certaine particulars as touching the first discoverie thereof, not commonly known, which discoverie al the writers of our time ascribe & that not unworthyily unto Christopher Columbus, For by him it was in a manner first discovered; made knowen, and profitably communicated unto the Christian world, in the yeere of our Lord 1492. Howbeit I finde that the North part thereof called Estotiland (which most of all extendeth toward our Europe and the Islands of the same, namely, Groneland, Island, and Frisland), was long ago found by certain fishers of the Isle of Frisland, driven by tempest upon the shore thereof: and was afterward about the year 1390 discovered a new, by one Antonio Zeno a gentleman of Venice; which sayled thither under the conduct of Zichmni king of saide Isle of Frisland, a prince in those parts of great valour, and renowned for his martiall exploits and victories. Of which expedition or abridgements gathered by Francisco Marcolino out of the letters of M. Nicolo and Antonio Zeni two gentlemen of Venice which lived in those parts. Out of which collections I doe adde concerning the description of Estotiland aforesaid these particulars following: Estotiland (saith he) aboundeth with all things necessary for mankinde. In the mids thereof standeth an exceeding high mountaine, from which issue foure rivers that moisten all the countrie. The inhabitants are wittie and most expert in all mechanical arts. They have a kinde of peculiar language and letters. Howbeit in this Kings Librarie are preserved certaine

Latine bookes, which they understand not, being perhaps left there not many years before by some Europeans, which traffiqued thither. They have all kinds of mettals; but especially golde, wherewith they mightly abound. They trafficke with the people of Groneland, from whence they fetch skinnes, pitch and brimstone. The inhabitants report that towardes the South, there are regions abounding with gold, and very populous. They have many and huge woods, from whence they take timber for the building of ships and cities whereof and of castles there are great store. The use of the loadstone for navigation is unknowen unto them.

"They make relation also of a certaine region toward the South, called Drogio, which is inhabited by Cannibals, unto whom mans flesh is delicate meat; whereof being destitute they live by fishing, which they use very much. Beyond this are large regions, and as it were a newe world: but the people are barbarous and goe naked; howbeit against the colde they cloth themselves in beastes skinnes. These have no kinde of metale; and they live by hunting. Their weapons are certaine long staves with sharpe points, and bowes. They wage warres one against another. They have governours, and obey certaine laves. But from hence more towardes the south the climate is much more temperate: and there are cities, and temples of idols, unto whom they sacrifice living men, whose flesh they afterwards devoure. These nations have the use of silver and gold.

"This much of this tract of landes out of the aforesaide collections or abridgements, wherein this also is worthy the observation that even then our European Pilots sayled those seas by the helpe of the loadstone. For concerning the use thereof in Navigation I suppose there is not to be found a more ancient testimonye. And these things I have annexed the rather unto this table of Mar del Zur; considering that none of those Authours which have written the Histories of the Newe World, heve in any part of their writings, mentioned one word thereof. Hitherto Ortelius."[7]

After these legendary voyages, innumerable fishermen, Basque, Spanish, Portuguese, Bretons, must have frequented this region for when the Cabotas or Cabots made their famous voyages, it is recorded that the fish, which nearly impeded the progress of their vessel, was called "baccaloa" by the natives. "Baccaloa" is found in old records and on ancient charts spelled in various ways.

When Francis Parkman was writing his *Pioneers of France in the New World*[8] he made an extensive search for the origin of this word, "baccaloa." He came to the conclusion that it was Basque, but that at an early period it had been adopted by the Spanish and Portuguese and always meant codfish. To have a word established in the mouths of natives surely signifies that fishermen in numbers and over a space of years must have caught codfish

[7] Hakluyt, 1928 ed., vol. 9, p. 355.

[8] Parkman, *Pioneers of France in the New World*, vol. 2, p. 9 n.

in these waters. The old Spanish is still spoken in Porto Rico and baccaloa, as they call codfish, is one of their chief articles of diet.

Bellet says the Basque had caught codfish (baccalaos) along the Newfoundland coast two hundred years before Columbus touched at Hispaniola.[9]

Hakluyt in his "Epistle Dedicatorie" to his *Divers Voyages,* in 1578, says:

"I marvaile not a little, that since the first discourie of America, which is now full fourscore and tenne years, after so great conquests and plantings of the Spaniards and Portingales there, that we of England could neur haue the grace to set fast footing in such fertill and temperate places as are left as yet unpossessed of them."

[9] Sylvester, *Sokaki Trail.*

CABOT AND HIS THREE SONS

From a drawing in the New York Public Library. EM4272

CHAPTER IV

JOHN CABOTA, or John Cabot, a Venetian cosmographer and navigator, went to Bristol, England, to found an establishment of maritime commerce. From various sources, but principally from the letters of the Spanish ambassador of that period, in England, it has been established that Cabot made several voyages to the west in search of the "Isle of Brezil" and the "Isle of the Seven Cities." On the fourth of these voyages he discovered the American continent at "Tierra de los Bacalloas," on the 24th day of June, 1494.[10]

He then had to have recourse to a sovereign to exercise authority, and he appealed to Henry VII of England. This was necessary as Columbus had discovered the West Indies and Pope Alexander VI had issued a papal bull adjudging the new world to Spain; but immediately after, when Portugal protested, established the famous line of demarkation between the territories of Spain and Portugal, which was confirmed at the treaty of Tordesillas, June 7, 1494.

The Portuguese, to whom fell this northern section, protested every undertaking such as the Cabots' after this. However, Henry VII, on March 5, 1496, signed letters-patent to John Cabot and three sons, Louis, Sebastian

[10] From a letter of M. D'Avezoc in *Me. Hist. Soc. Coll. Doc. Hist.*, ser. 2, vol. 1.

and Sancius. They did not put to sea until May of 1497. An account of this voyage was sent by Lorenzo Pasqualigo, a Venetian merchant, from London to his brother in Venice, containing what he had learned of the results of this voyage:

"John Cabot had found at a distance of seven hundred leagues in the west, a firm land, along which he had coasted for the space of three hundred leagues, not having met a living person at the points where he had landed, but still having observed there some traces of inhabitants, trees notched, and nets for catching game; on his return, he had seen on his right hand two islands, where, however, he had not wished to go on shore on account of the failure of his provisions: he returned to Bristol, after a voyage of three months, having left in the lands which he had discovered a grand cross, with the banner of England and that of St. Mark of Venice.

This land appears to have been the same that was later discovered by Gomez.

Where Cabot stopped, his first landfall and where he erected the great cross, are still debatable points. Monhegan might as easily have been the place as the present Newfoundland.

There is an amusing bear story told in records of this voyage:

"Cabot and his Companions took a great deal of Pleasure in seeing the Bears hunt these fish (The fish Baccalai) which they did in the following manner. There are upon these Coasts many Large Trees, whose leaves falling into the Waters, the Fish come and snap at them greedily. The Bears, who have no other Food here, observing this, lay themselves in Ambuscade to catch them. As soon as the Fish lift their Heads above Water to get the Leaves, the Bears throw in their Claws, and if they can but grapple them under their Scales, they will be sure to bring them to Land. But some great Fish have been known to drag the Bears into the Water by meer force, when there has happen'd a very diverting Combat between them; sometimes one's uppermost, and then the other, but it generally happens the Bear gets the better and brings the Fish to Land and devours him. These Bears are by no means dangerous, nor do any manner of harm to the Inhabitants."[11]

Bears in this section, on the mainland, were very numerous during the early days of the settlers, as many tales are to be found of their antics and depredations on the little plantations of Indian corn.

Wonderful tales of queer creatures and monsters enlivened the tales of voyagers. Hakluyt tells a good one about the whales that were to be encountered:

"There be seen sometimes neere into Island huge whales like unto mountains, which overturne ships, unlesse they be terrified, or beguiled with rond and emptie vessels, which they delight to tosse up and down. It sometimes

[11] Du Perier, *General history of all voyages and travels throughout the old and new world.* London, 1708.

falleth out that Mariners thinking these whales to be Ilands, and casting our ankers upon their backs, are often in danger of drowning."[12]

The Spanish became very much excited over the Cabot voyages and their Ambassador at London sent the following dispatch to the King:

"The news that fishing banks could be reached after 'a voyage of not more than fifteen days,' where 'the sea is covered with cod-fish, which are caught in vast numbers simply by driving a basket into the waters.'"[13]

The Spanish organized a governing body for this new territory called "America Septrentrionalle." A notation on a Spanish map gives the scheme of control:

"America Seprentrionalle" was to be governed by the, "Vice-Roy de Mexico, un Captaine General, un President, un Marchal de Camp, un Commandant General d'l'Equipage, huitt counseilers and plusiers autres officers," according to the legend on an ancient Spanish map in the Boston Library.

Again Henry VII signed letters-patent to John Cabot, after his return with this news of a continent to the west in 1498. For some reason, perhaps the death of John Cabot, Sebastian probably took command of the expedition, which consisted of five ships. This voyage was not a success, although they sailed from 58° N. L. southward

[12] Hakluyt, *Breife Commentarie on the true State of Island.*

[13] Dispatches of Pedro de Ayala, July 25, 1498, in Brown's *Genesis of the United States.*

to 36°. He may have put in to Monhegan on this trip south. Finally Sebastian Cabot made a fourth voyage, advancing as far north as 67° 30′ N. L. These voyages had as their object a passage to Cathay.

The Cosa map combines the information obtained by Columbus, and the Cabots, and is the best and oldest map of the East Coast of North America. It was made by Juan de la Cosa, at Puerto de Sta. Maria, one of the most ancient settlements on the Bay of Cádiz, in 1500. Monhegan is probably the dot on this map opposite the Cavo de St. Jorge (George).

Sebastian Cabot[14] immediately on his return from this voyage went to Spain where he was appointed Pilot-Major, by royal decree on February 5, 1518. He was at the council of Badajoz, in 1524, where the voyages to our northeast coast must have been constantly mooted, as the intended expedition of Estavam Gomez to discover the Northwest Passage depended greatly on the ruling of this council.

But the Cabot voyages firmly fixed the English claim to the northeastern shores of North America, which up to that time they had only held through the Madock or Welsh tradition.

During these years the fishermen were flocking to the

[14] Sebastian Cabot tried to sell, or sold, so the story runs, to Venice and to England the pretended "Secret of the Strait," and certain cosmographers of Charles V, flattered themselves that they knew of a short route to Molucca, or the Spice Islands.

cod grounds. In 1527 an English captain reported that he found in the harbor of St. John, Newfoundland, alone, 11 Norman, 1 Breton and 2 Portuguese sails.

The great publicity given to Columbus' discovery of the West Indies and the tremendous conquests by the Spanish in Mexico and South America, with the attendant fabulous tales of gold, silver, pearls, and precious stones—looted wealth of the ancient races of America, substantiated by the capture of the richly laden ships, homeward bound, by the French, English and other maritime nations—stirred the imagination and aroused the greedy avarice of the war-poor monarchs of Europe.

In the tremendous struggle between Catholicism and Protestantism, which was going on at this time, Charles V, of Spain, with plans for world dominion in his head, Henry VIII, of England, quarreling with the Pope, and François I, of France, wanting power and money; hatreds and jealousies were started in Europe that continued during the centuries when America was becoming known to the world. These quarrels and wranglings were inherited by Queen Elizabeth and Phillip II of Spain. During this period two powerful Popes, Alexander VI of the Borgia family, and Clement VII of the Medici family, were in temporal power at the Vatican.

The hatreds so engendered, between these powerful monarchs, put a premium on secrecy regarding any movement toward the exploration and the colonization of America, both north and south. The desire for spiritual control of the new continents and their inhabitants added to the animosities of the time.

At the same time the Spanish Inquisition was in full swing and to destroy and plunder anything Spanish was thought to be an act directed by God. The renaissance of literature, art and science, too, was at its height during this momentous period. All of Europe was stirring, and the greatest heights of achievement in every line seem to have been crowded into these two centuries, during which the discovery and settlement of America coincide. Hatred, jealousy, greed, superstition, cruelty and secrecy were the results.

Due to the strict *espionnage* kept up by the Spanish at London, many of the documents and most of the important charts which have to do with the English explorations in the North Atlantic have been found tucked away in the archives of Spain, and some also in France. Secrecy was the main of the many reasons why it has been so difficult for historians and cartographers to get records and charts of the early voyages, and to locate places accurately.

Then, too, there were many rival groups of merchant adventurers in Holland and England. These groups were rarely willing to disclose to competitors the places where they obtained their rich cargoes of furs and fish.

Fishermen were also rather reticent as to where they made their catches. They were not men of learning, and did not write accounts of their voyages, nor did they draw maps of their fishing havens.

How the French felt toward the Spanish is illustrated in the statement of Lescarbot:

"Considering which, we may justly curse the houre that greedie avarice did carrie the Spaniard into the West, for the woful events that have ensued thereof — For when I consider that by his greedinesse he hath kindled and mantayned the warre throwall Christendome, and his only studie hath beene how to destroy his neighbors (and not the Turke) I cannot thinke that any other but the Devill hath beene the Authour of their voyages."

All through every period of Monhegan's history the pirates and corsairs, of one nationality or another, made each voyage a great hazard, both for those that sailed and those who adventured their money in these enterprises.

Henry VIII of England, while very busy with his numerous wives and his quarrel with the Pope, still seems to have found time to authorize an expedition by Master John Rut to discover a Northwest Passage in 1527. Various historians claim that Verrazano accompanied Rut on this voyage and that he was killed by the natives and buried on the shores of Norumbega. This is doubtful. There is an account that Henry VIII, Michael Lok, and Richard Hakluyt, looked at a "mightie large olde mappe." This would seem to have been Verrazano's map with Italian names all along the coast of North America. De Costa has deciphered most of them.

CHAPTER V

BETWEEN the last voyage of Sebastian Cabot and that of Gomez, in 1524, the Portuguese had sent out three expeditions in search of a Northwest Passage. The first of these expeditions was conducted by Gaspar Corte-Reals. Gaspar's father, John Vaz Corte-Reals, had been made Governor of Terceira, one of the Azores, and some historians claim that he had made a voyage of discovery to an island called "Terre de Baccalhaos" (land of cod-fish), but this has not been reliably credited as yet. Harrisse[15] thinks there is reason to believe that the Portuguese reached the American continent as early as 1474, or even ten years earlier.

Gaspar Corte-Reals started from Lisbon in 1500, stopping at the Azores, where his brother Vasqueases, had succeeded his father as governor, and reached land which he called Terre Verde, or Green-land. According to Kohl, he made another trip in 1501, with two vessels. His landfall was probably Newfoundland, he then steered northward and encountered so much ice that he returned to the south. Somewhere on the trip southerly he seized upon fifty-seven natives. He put fifty of them in his own boat and seven in his consort. The description of these natives is such that they must have been Indians and not Esqui-

[15] Harrisse (Les Cortereal, 27).

maux. The consort arrived at Lisbon in October of 1501, but Corte-Reals was never heard of again.

They brought home beside the seven natives "a piece of a gilded sword of Italian workmanship, and two silver ear-rings which they had found in the possession of the aborigines." "There can be scarcely a doubt," says Kohl, "that these interesting objects had been left there by the the Cabots who, some years before had visited the same region." They may, however, have been left by the Portuguese or Spanish captains and discoverers whose voyages are not recorded, or have not come to light.

Miguel Corte-Reals, a younger brother, went in search of his brother Gaspar the following spring and he never returned or was heard of afterwards. King Emanuel of Portugal then sent out another searching expedition for the brothers in 1503 consisting of two vessels, which after an unsuccessful cruise returned without news. It is quite possible that in the search for the lost brothers that the coast of Maine might have been passed, which of course would mean that they sighted, at least, Monhegan.

The Cantino map is supposed to contain the information obtained by the Corte-Reals voyages.

During this misty historical period the French, whose hardy Normans, Breton and Basque fishermen had been making yearly voyages to the cod fisheries, became interested in this new country. They even claim that the Frenchman, Cousin, or Cossin, first discovered America.

"Cousin, a navigator of Dieppe, being at sea off the

African coast, was forced westward, it is said by winds and currents, to within sight of an unknown shore, where he presently described the mouth of a great river. On board his ship was one Pinzon, whose conduct became so mutinous that, on his return to Dieppe, Cousin made complaint to the magistracy, who thereupon dismissed the offender from the maritime service of the town. Pinzon went to Spain, became known to Columbus, told him the discovery, and joined him on his voyage of 1492."[16]

The French are also said to have had a pilot from St. Jean de Luz who first discovered America. In 1565 Charles IX, of France, informed the Spanish Ambassador that the coast of North America had been discovered by French subjects more than a hundred years before, and gave as evidence the name of "Terre aux Bretons," found on old maps, which has to this day continued as the name for one of the capes.

Jean Dénys was supposed to have visited these regions, as well as Thomaso Aubert,[17] a navigator who came in 1508 and took Indians from Canada to France. Some of these Indians were portrayed in Dieppe and appear amongst other figures in an old piece of masonry or bas-relief, still preserved in the Church of St. James in Dieppe.[18]

16 Parkman, *Pioneers of France in the New World*, vol. 2, p. 8.

17 Ramusio, III, 423.

18 Vitet, *Histoire de Dieppe*, p. 112.

In 1517 there were said to have been one hundred and fifty French fishing vessels in Newfoundland during the season.

From Drake's *History of Boston*, p. 4

While the voyages of the Cabots was the English gesture toward claiming the new world, the expedition of Verrazano was the basis of the claims of the French. François I, the picturesque and beauty-loving king of France, sponsored this voyage. Verrazano was an Italian (a Venetian), who like other of his illustrious countrymen found a patron who appreciated merit, and he was sent out in 1523 for the discovery of *terra nuova.*

His voyage is well recorded, and we find him ranging the coast in the *Dauphine* in 1524. The following item shows he must have inspected our island, along with the others on the coast of Maine, as he sailed northward:

"Continuing directly along the coast for the space of fifty leagues, we discovered 32 Islands, lying all neere the land, being small and pleasant to the view, high, and having many turnings and windings between them, making many harbourghs and channels as they do in the gulfe of Venice, in Sclavonia and Dalmatia."[19]

Verrazano was apparently the first voyager to discover Norumbega, the mysterious El Dorado region sought for by voyagers for the next century and a half. It is laid down on the map made from his voyage in this region and he spells it Aranbega. He tells of a native blessing them:

"He stopped as if astonished and prayed, worshipping like a monk, lifting his finger toward the sky, and pointing to the sea he appeared to bless us."

This name Norumbega, in its various spellings, is the key to locating Monhegan in the voyages and on charts, for our Island was in the path of all voyagers to that region.

[19] Hakluyt's translation from Ramusio, in *Divers Voyages,* 1582.

CHAPTER VI

THE next official voyager to the region of Monhegan was Estevan Gomez, an experienced Portuguese pilot, employed by Charles V, King of Spain. He was one of the members of the Council of Badajos where he must have had close relationship with not only Sebastian Cabot, but with Juan Vespucci, Diego Ribero and other celebrated pilots and cosmographers. This council was to settle disagreements between Spain and Portugal as to the division of territory in the new world.

Armed with probably more information than any other voyager of those times, he sailed in 1525. No detailed record of his voyage remains or has been as yet unearthed. The knowledge of his explorations that has come down is taken from charts, principally from that of Ribero, made in 1529. On this chart the coast of Maine is called "La tierra de Gomez" (The Land of Gomez). The "c.d. muchas yslas" (Cape of Many Islands) is apparently Owl's Head. The Penobscot he named "Rio Grande" (Great River), and the "Archipelago de Estevan Gomez" seems to have included the group of islands in the Gulf of Maine.

There is also a map made by Alonzo de Santa Cruz in *Islario* which is supposed to contain the information obtained by Gomez, which shows an island marked by a cross which is in the general location of Monhegan.

What the old cartographers meant by a cross on the maps, is not definitely known, but probably it indicated a harbor fit for vessels.

João Alvarez Fagundes, a Portuguese mariner who established codfisheries near "Cabo Bretaõ" that brought great profit to Portugal, was near Monhegan in 1520 and he may have given it one of the names that he gave to the islands in this vicinity: Santo Anthonio, 11000 Virgins, Islands of Santa Cruz, etc.

Again François I was persuaded to father a voyage to the new lands. This was that of Jacques Cartier who left St. Malo in April of 1534. He explored the St. Lawrence River principally, returning to France with two Indians that he had captured.

The next year he again left St. Malo, May 19, 1535, sailed directly to the St. Lawrence; named Canada, located Hochelaga, and spent the winter in a harbor, called by him "Holy Cross," which was on the River of Hochelaga (St. Lawrence). His crew suffered from scurvy, of which disease he lost twenty-five of his company and would have lost more had not the friendly natives checked it by means of a decoction of leaves from a tree called by them *ameda.*

Again he captured an Indian Chief, Dannacona, and some of his subjects, and sailed away to France. On his return times were unpropitious for another voyage and it was not until 1540 that another French expedition was got under way. This time the expedition was headed by Roberval and was purported to be one of colonization and for the conversion of the ungodly natives.

Cartier was the commander of the ship which not only carried priests but women as well as men. Roberval was given the title of "Lord of Norembegue and the regions north of 40°." This expedition left St. Malo the 23rd of May, 1541. Donnacona and his subjects had in the meantime died in France, so on Cartier's return he was received with extreme hostility by the Indians.

From a French map of 1543 we have the discoveries of Cartier depicted, while the name of the region is given as Aurobague. A small castle occupies a position at the head of the Penobscot, while islands are dotted all along the coast.

Another French map, published a year or so later, shows Owl's Head as "C. de la Croix" (Cape of the Cross), while many islands are shown scattered about the mouth of "Rio de gamas" (Deer River). Drawings of European men and women decorate the country discovered by Cartier.

Cartier brought back from his explorations reports not only of a land peopled by a race of one-legged folk (unapied), most probably seals, but also of a region in those parts where the people were "as white as those of France."

The year before, or 1540, Diego Maldonado in his searching expedition to find the lost De Sota, made a minute survey of the whole eastern coast of North America as far as the country of the "Bacallaos." As he spent a year in this painful task there can be little doubt that he looked over Monhegan's harbor for a trace of his chief.

Gómara, the Spanish historian, in 1553 says, "that many voyages of discovery had been made to the Western Indies, particularly to the North, of which we have received no word."[20]

In 1556 Monhegan Island is probably described for the first time. André Thevet, a French Huguenot, who went with the Protestant colony to Brazil, and who was a celebrated traveler and cosmographer, on his return from that colonization scheme, took passage on a vessel which sailed along the entire coast of "Florida," as the whole coast of North America was sometimes then called. In his *Cosmographie Universelle*, which he wrote after his return, he gives the following description of the region of Norumbega, which name Verrazano had fastened on the region of the Penobscot and by which it was known for one hundred and fifty years:

"Having left La Florida on the left hand, with all its islands, gulfs and capes, a river presents itself, which is one of the finest rivers in the whole world, which we call 'Norumbegue,' and the aborigines Agoncy; and which is marked on some mariners charts as the Grand River. Several other beautiful rivers enter into it; and upon its banks the French formerly erected a little fort about ten or twelve leagues from its mouth, which was surrounded

[20] Gómara, *Historia General de las Indies*, fol. 2.

by fresh water, and this place was named the Fort of Norumbegue. . . ."

"Before you enter the said river appears an island (Monhegan) surrounded by eight very small islets, which are near the country of the Green Mountains (Camden Hills), and to the Cape of islets (Cabo de muchas islas). From there you sail all along unto the mouth of the river, which is dangerous from the great number of thick and high rocks, and its entrance is wonderfully large."

The first English description of Monhegan was made by David Ingram, a sailor on Capt. John Hawkins' famous expedition to the Spanish Main. During October of 1568 Ingram was marooned by Captain Hawkins along with a hundred other companions on the shores of the Gulf of Mexico. Hawkins was forced to this extreme measure on account of lack of ships and provisions. Most of the sailors or soldiers wended their way southward, but David Ingram with two of his companions started north, probably knowing of the annual visits of fishing vessels to the coasts of Norumbega. They traveled afoot on the Indian trails along the whole east coast of the United States, and finally in the region of the "River Garinda which is 60 leagues west from Cape Breton," thought by some to be the St. John's River, they embarked on a French ship, the *Gargarine,* commanded by Captain Champagne, and sailed away to Newhaven (Havre), France in 1569. The river Garinda was probably the Penobscot.*

* David Ingram had been on the fateful voyage of Sir Humphrey Gilbert in 1583, according to George Peckham. Found in Mag. of Hist., No. 68, 1920.

On this trip, which he described in such a vivid way, and so came to the notice of Hakluyt, he saw Monhegan from a distance as the following, quoted from his relation in a court of law, testifies:

"Taking me into his canoa, we paddled across eastward from the place he called Sabino to a peninsula which he called Pemcuit, and where we rested over that night. When the morning broke, I saw not far to seaward, a great island that was backed like a whale. I first took it for a whale, as those fish in that country are easily taken for islands at a distance, so high do their backs rear out of the sea, and so enormous are they that one would load a hundred ships. The Sagamo said it was an island and that the people who lived on it were subjects of the Bashaba." *

In early colonial times Sabino and Pemcuit were familiar words. Pemaquid Point was sometimes called Pemcuit, and we will hear more of the Bashaba from the Gorges' *Relation* later.

Ingram evidently reached the seat of the Bashaba and saw the city of Bega, as he called it, where buckets of pearls, pillars of crystal and silver and its great wealth of peltry dazzled his eyes to his later undoing and the court of law.

At any rate his story put Norumbega on the English map for a century to come. This city of Bega was probably the one Verrazano called Aranbega, and was undoubtedly near the site of the present city of Bangor.

* Sylvester's *Land of Castine.*

From this time forth Monhegan became the landmark for the fair country of Norumbega which to the English captains of Elizabeth appeared another country like unto the Spanish conquest with Inca treasures of gold; and the outpost for the discovery of the northwest passage to Cathay, as the northern route across the ocean had not been charted as yet.

Peaceful possession by the English seems to have been taken of these shores, by the year 1574, for we have confirming this a statement which was contained in a letter from the Spanish Ambassador to England, Don Pedro de Zùniga, to the King of Spain, on the subject of Virginia: ". . . and it having been seen in the Council that the Condestable of Castile (Juan Ferdinand de Velasco) has reported that when he was negotiating the Treaty of Peace in England (August 19, 1604), he considered that if particularly anxious to treat of the excluding the English from the Indies and more especially from Virginia (another name for all the east coast at that time), he would have to encounter the difficulty that it is more than 30 years since they have had peaceful possession of it and that, if it were declared that Virginia was not a part of the Indies, a very dangerous door would be opened."[21]

Where the English held peaceful possession has not come to light. It is undoubtedly possible that some English fishing crews were even then spending the winters on

[21] Brown, *Genesis of the United States,* vol. 1, p. 126.

COD-FISHING INDUSTRY IN EARLY TIMES
From Moll's Map, 1700. New York Public Library, Map Room

Monhegan. Newfoundland was the general term for all these fishing grounds at that period.

That the Spanish decided that this latitude was unfavorable for colonization by them seems evident. There is a notation regarding this:

"And whensoever afterwardes the Spanish (very proper in all their Southerne discoveries) did attempt any thing into Florida and those regions inclining toward the North they proved most unhappy, and were at length discouraged utterly by the hard and lamentable successes of many bothe religious and valiant in armes, endearvering to bring these Northerly regions also under the Spanish jurisdiction as if God had prescribed limits unto the Spanish nation which they might not exceed; as by their own gests recorded may be aptly gathered."[22]

As the fishing industry is of especial importance to our history, a letter written from Newfoundland in 1578[23] by A. Parkhurst is unusually interesting as it describes the fishing fleets:

"Now to answer some part of your letter touching the sundry navies that come to Newfoundland, or Terra Nova, for fish: you shal understand that some fish not neere the other by 200 leagues, and therefore the certaintie is not known; and some yeres come many more than

[22] "Sir Humphrey Gilbert's Voyage to Newfoundland," *Old South Leaflets*, 118, vol. 5, p. 351.

[23] A letter written to M. Richard Hakluyt of the Middle Temple, containing a report of the true state and commodities of Newfoundland, by M. Anthonie Parkhurst, Gentleman, 1578.

others come, as I see the like among us: who since my first travell being but 4 yeeres, are increased from 30 sayle to 56. which commeth to passe chiefly by the imagination of the Westerne men, who thinke their neighborers have had greater gaines then in very deed they have, for that they see me to take such secret commoditie by reason that I doe search the harbors, creekes and havens, and also the land much more then ever any Englishman hath done. Surely I am glad that it so increaseth. But to let this passe, you shall understand that I am informed that there are above 100 saile of Spaniards that come to take cod (who make all wet and do drie it when they come home) besides 20. or 30. more that come from Biskaie to kill Whale for Traine. These be better appoynted for shipping and furniture of munitions, then any nation saving the Englishmen, who commonly are lords of the harbors where they fish, and do use all strangers helpe in fishing if need require, according to an old custome of the country, which thing they do willingly, so that you take noting from them more then a boat or twaine of salt, in respect of your protection of them against rovers or other violent intruders, who do often put them from good harbor etc. As touching their tunnage, I thinke it may be neere five or six thousand tunne. But of Portugals there are not lightly above 50 saile, and they make all wet in like sorte, whose tunnage may amount to three thousand tuns, and not upwarde. Of the French nation and Britons, are about one hundred and fiftie sailes and most of their shipping is very small, not past forty tunnes, among which some are great and reasonably well appointed, better than the Portuguls, and not so well as the Spaniards, and the burden of them may be some 7000 tunne. Their shipping is from all parts of France and Britaine (Brittany), and the Spaniards from most parts of Spaine, and the Portugals from Aviero and Iana and from 2 or 3 ports more. The trade that our nation hath to Island (Iceland) maketh, that the English are not there in such numbers as other nations. . . ."

Mr. Parkhurst's letter contains other interesting items among which is this:

"Muskles, in which I have found pearles above 40 in one muskle, and generally all have some, great or small. I heard of a Portugall that found one woorth 300 duckets."

This confirms Ingram's story in regard to the great store of pearls. Another item is of interest to Monhegan: "I finde salt kerned on the rockes in nine and fortie and better: there places may bee found for salt in three and fortie."

Stephen Bellinger, of Rouen, "who founde a towne conteyninge fourscore houses and returned home, with a diligent description of the coast in the space of four months, with many commodities of the countrie, which he showed me. This was in the Norumbega country. . . . For this coast is never subject to the ise, which is never lightly seene to the south of Cape Razo in New founde lande."

This testimony is only one of many to be found in Hakluyt's tales of voyages to this part of Maine.

Capt. Richard Whithorne voyaged to these regions in 1579, according to Brown.[24]

In Hakluyt's *Westerne Planting* by Peckham there is an item of interest about the Indians of this region at that time, and formerly:

"Seinge that the people of that parte of America from 30 degrees in Florida Northwarde unto 63 degrees (which ys yet in no Christian princes actuall possession) are idolaters; and that those which Stephen Gomes broughte from the coaste of Norumbega in the yere 1524 worshipped the sonne, the moone, and the starres, and used other idolatrie, as it ys recorded in the historie of Gonsuluo de Ouido, in Italian, fol. 52 of the third volume of Ramusius and that those of Canada and Hochelaga in 48, & 50 degrees worshippe a spirite which they call Cudruaigny, as we reade in the tenthe chapiter of the second relation of Jacques Cartier, . . ."

[24] Brown, *Genesis of the United States.*

CHAPTER VII

To understand aright the close relationship existing among the many English adventurers to this new world a study of Dr. Dee's Diary will be helpful.

Dr. Dee was an English mathematician, astrologer, cartographer and necromancer to Queen Elizabeth. He was an early favorite with the Queen and it may well be that he was the force instrumental in directing her efforts toward the schemes of colonization and of discovery in these parts of the elusive Northwest Passage. No complete history of his life has come to hand in this research for information regarding Monhegan's place in these efforts. His map (1580) of the New World has a cross at the place where Monhegan should be.

Dr. Dee was consulted by Lord Dudley to name a propitious day for the coronation of Queen Elizabeth. His prophesy must have been fortunate, for it was on Coronation Day that he was presented to the Queen, who became so interested in him that she took lessons in the mystical interpretations of his writings. Under her favor he studied and made a great collection of curious books, manuscripts and unusual instruments, at his home at Mortlake.

In 1578 Queen Elizabeth had an illness and he was sent abroad to consult with German physicians and astrologers in regard to it. On his return he was immediately employed in investigating the Queen's title to the now famous new world and in furnishing geographical descriptions. In these ways he became a most important personage at the Court, one to be reckoned with by peo-

ple interested in expeditions to the short route to the "Spice Lands of Cathai." We find, therefore, that all the persons connected with these enterprises, from 1578 to 1595, to have been anxious for his favor and desiring his advice, as the following extracts from his Diary indicate:

"Nov. 28, 1578. I declared to the Queene her title to Greenland, Estetiland and Friseland."

Two large rolls containing this information are still extant in the Cottonian Library. The word "Estetiland" appearing here would seem to indicate that Dr. Dee had access to the Zeno charts or possibly some of the old Norse maps as the word also appears on them. Undoubtedly he had the Welsh material as well as the Cabots' reports of their voyages. It is in 1578 also that Sir Humphrey Gilbert obtained an extensive grant of land in the new found land from 30° to 40° of North Latitude.

"June 3, 1579, Mr. A. Gilbert and J. Davys rod homeward into Devonshire."

Mr. A. Gilbert was the brother of Sir Humphrey Gilbert and John Davis was probably John Davis the discoverer of Davis Strait. The English were starting in earnest.

Of these English captains the first to come was Simon Ferdinando, in a "little frigate" in the service of Walsingham, in 1579. In 1580 we find that John Walker, in the service of Sir Humphrey Gilbert, conducted a voyage to the River of Norumbega.

"He reached the Penobscot, of which he gave a rough description, finding the region rich in furs, as described by Alfonsee and Ingram. He discovered a silver mine where modern industry is now every year opening new veins of silver and gold. This voyage like that of his predecessor, proved a short one, — the return trip being made direct to France, where 'hides,' which he had secured were sold for forty shillings apiece."[25]

Undoubtedly he stopped at Monhegan as the island by this time must have been fairly well known.

From Dee's Diary we have:

"Sept. 10, 1580. Sir Humfry Gilbert granted me my request to him, made by letter, for royalties of discovery

[25] De Costa in Windsor's *Narrative and Critical History of America*, Section "Norumbega and Its English Explorers."

all to the north above the parallell of the 50° of latitude, in the presence of Stoner, Sir John Gilbert, his servant and retainer; and thereupon toke me by the hand with faithful promises in his lodging of John Cooke's house in Wichcross stres, where we dyned onely us three together, being Satterday."

Evidently Dee had his eye out for some returns for his information, advice and patronage. This entry also shows that Dee must have influenced Sir Humphrey in regard to the value of the northern country, for in Hakluyt's tale of "The Manner how the Sayd Admirall was lost, 1583," he says: "Herein my opinion was better confirmed diversly, and by sundry conjectures, which maketh me have the greatre hope of this rich Mine. For where as the Generall (Sir Humphrey) had never before a good conceit of the North parts of the world: now his mind was wholly fixed upon the New found land. And as before he refused not to grant assignements liberally to them that required the same into these North parts, now he became contrarily affected, refusing to make any so large grants, especially of St. Johns, which certaine English merchants made suite for, offering to employ their money and travell upon the same: yet neither by their owne suite, nor of others of his owne company, whom he seemed willing to pleasure, it could be obtained.

"Also laying downe his determination, in the Spring following, for desposing of his voyage then to be reattempted: he assigned the Captaine & Master of the *Gold-*

en Hind, unto the South discovery, and reserved unto himselfe the North, affirming that this voyage had woune his heart from the South, and that now he was become a Northern man altogether."

Again, Dee's Diary notes:

"June 17, 1581, Young Mr. Hawkins, who had been with Sir Francis Drake cam to me at Mortlake."

This Mr. Hawkins was undoubtedly the son of Sir John Hawkins, the Armada hero, who was then about twenty years of age.

"Jan. 23, 1582, The Right Honorable Mr. Secretary Walsingham cam to my house, where by good lok he found Mr. Awdrian Gilbert, and so talk was begonne of Northwest Straights discovery."

The next day they had another talk. At this time the Spanish were asserting their claim to the whole of North America as high as Labrador, under the name of "Florida," and Don Pedro Menendez de Aviles, in establishing his "Province of Florida," is supposed to have surveyed the whole coast of Maine and to have visited Monhegan. He had his eye on the Banks of Newfoundland and intended to protect the Spanish fishermen in these waters.

"Jan. 24, 1582. I, Mr. Awdrian Gilbert, John Davis went by appointment to Mr. Secretary (Walsingham) to Mr. Beale, his house, where we four were secret, and we made Mr. Secretary privie of the N. W. passage, and all charts and rutters (routes) were again agreed uppon in general."

"July 16, 1582. A meridie hor. 3½ cam Sir. George Peckham to me to know the tytle for Norembega in respect of Spayn and Portugall parting the whole world's distilleryes. He promised me of his gift and of his patient . . . of the new conquest, and thought to get so moche of Mr. Gerardes gift to be sent me with seale within a few days."

This item would seem to indicate that Peckham believed in Norumbegua's wealth, and the determination of the English to contest the old line of demarkation between Spanish and Portuguese territory established by the Pope in 1494 and also that Sir George Peckham and Mr. Gerrades (Sir Thomas Gerrard) were recipients of some of the Spanish gold looted from treasure ships traveling from the land of the "rich Caribees" to Cádiz. Sir George Peckham, an ardent Catholic, was one of the chief adventurers in the expedition of Sir Humphrey Gilbert. To Gerrard and Peckham, Sir Humphrey had assigned his patent.

"Aug. 31, 1582. Benjamin Lok told me of his father's mynde to send him to Spayn within three or four days."

Benjamin Lok was the son of Michael Lok who made a map about this time, in which most of the Verrazano and Cartier discoveries are laid down. His map has several large islands at the entrance of the River of Norumbega (Penobscot). One is probably intended for Monhegan. It appears that information as to Spanish voyages and charts is wanted and Benjamin is to be sent in search

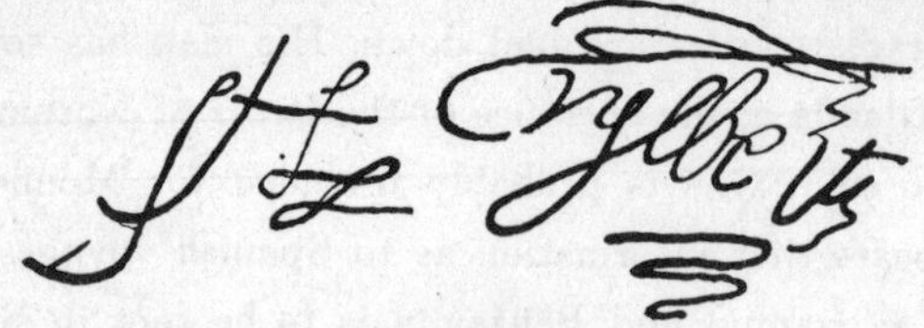

SIR HUMPHREY GILBERT

From the *Heroologia Anglica* of Henry Holland

"Nov. 1, 1582. The same day cam Mr. Clement the sea master and Mr. Ingram from Sir George Peckham."

This Mr. Ingram is evidently the sailor David Ingram, whose description of buckets of pearls, houses covered with copper, with pillars of crystal, and great store of peltry at Bega, set afire the desire of the English adventurers for this treasure. Sir George Peckham was one of Ingram's examiners when he was under oath in regard to his experiences.

Supposedly two years before Dr. Dee had published his map and on it is a cross near the location of Monhegan, the whale island of Ingram's tale.

So secretive were the English explorers of this time that Sir Humphrey Gilbert took unusual precaution in regard to concealing the sailing directions of his voyage. In the winter before the voyage, Gilbert had carefully selected watchwords to be used, upon the voyage, and had sealed them up in two bullets or scowles. The bullet sealed with the yellow wax was to be opened immediately and contained the sailing directions for the English and Irish coasts. The one sealed with red wax was only to be opened after these coasts were left behind. He also arranged a code of signals by means of flags in the daytime and of lights by night.[26]

"Mar. 6, 1583. I, and Mr. Adrian Gilbert and John

[26] There is a "Relation of Richard Clarke of Weymouth, master of the ship called *The Delight* going for the discovery of Norembega, with Sir Humphrey Gilbert, 1583."

Davis did mete with Mr. Alderman Barnes, Mr. Thonson and Mr. Young and Mr. Hudson about the Northwest passage."

Henry Hudson is evidently the Mr. Hudson here spoken of. Adrian Gilbert had a patent for the Northwest Passage.

"Mar. 17, 1583. Mr. John Davys went to Chelsey with Mr. Adrian Gilbert to Mr. Radforths, and so the 18th day from thence to Devonshyre."

John Davis was probably getting ready for his great expedition which terminated in the discovery of Davis Straight in 1585.

"May 4, 1583. Mr. Adrian Gilbert and Mr. Repler went by water to Braynford, and so to ride to Devonshire."

There is a lapse here of several years in the "Diary," as published. It may have been due to the overthrow of Sir Humphrey's voyage.

Sir Humphrey Gilbert had written a "Discourse of a North-West Passage," in 1566, which was published without his authority, it is stated, in 1576. In this document he quotes the experience, "of our yeerly fishers to Labador and Terra Nova." He knew the fishermen and had questioned them and had learned all that they could tell him of the waters they frequented. In 1583 Sir Humphrey took possession of Newfoundland, and afterwards sailed for Norumbega, whither his "man" Walker had gone three years before. As Monhegan was the outpost for Norumbega, we can be sure that Gilbert visited it. Dee, who knew enough about it to make a cross on his map at its location, was evidently constantly consulted by Gilbert's backers. How Sir Humphrey was lost is known to every reader and we will not retell it here.

According to Sewall it is at this time "Monhegan earliest appears in the panorama of the historic scene of English life and enterprise on the New England shores."

"Pedro Mendez, Governor of Florida, in despatches forwarded by him to the Court of Spain, tells Phillip II, 'that in July of the year (1588) that English were inhabiting an island in latitude 43°, eight leagues from the land, where the Indians are very numerous.'[27] This was the story of Carlos Morea, a Spaniard who had learned the facts in London and communicated them to Mendez."

No doubt that Monhegan was the island so occupied by these English dwellers in the New World.

Sir Bernard Drake (eldest son of John Drake, had a sister who was the first wife of Walter Raleigh) was knighted by Queen Elizabeth January 9, 1586. On his return from a voyage to Newfoundland he took many Portuguese ships laden with fish from Newfoundland and carried them home to England as prizes. While on this voyage he is supposed to have stopped at Monhegan.

Sir Francis Drake landed on the coast of New England in 1586 and spent a few days in trading. He was returning to England from a trip to the West Indies. He probably stopped in our harbor.

[27] Brown, *Genesis of the United States*, p. 880.

In 1588 the Invincible Armada of Philip II was destroyed, by a tempest, and Drake, Raleigh and Elizabeth's other captains commenced privateering and conquering right and left. The Gilbert-Raleigh family must have come in for considerable plunder for under date of December 29, 1589, in Dee's Diary, we find Dee being recompensed:

"Dec. 29, 1589. Mr. Adrian Gilbert cam to me at Mortlak, and offered me as much as I could require at his hands, both for my goods carried away and for the mynes."

Evidently Dr. Dee had ventured his goods with Sir Humphrey Gilbert's ill-fated voyage or perhaps a later expedition connected with Raleigh. Adrian Gilbert was Sir Humphrey Gilbert's own brother, and he was half brother to Sir Walter Raleigh.

"Oct. 9, 1595. I dined with Sir Walter Rawlegh at Durham House."

This is the last entry concerning voyages in the Diary. Dee's influence with the Queen and explorers seems to have waned. He finally came under suspicion, was driven from his house, and his wonderful library destroyed. This destruction may account for the loss of many valuable maps and documents concerning our early history, which historians have sought so long in vain.

The elder Hakluyt must have had a very good idea of this region of Norumbega, for he not only printed Ingram's tale, but he published a map by Molyneaux on

SIR WALTER RALEIGH
From New York Public Library. EM1690

which the copper mines off the eastern coast of Maine at Menan were indicated.

The next English voyager of record seems to have been Richard Strong, who in 1593 sailed to Cape Breton, and afterwards cruised some time "up and down the coast of 'Arembec' to the west and south-west of Cape Breton." He reported rather vaguely that he saw men whom he judged to be Christians, "sailing in boats to the southwest of Cape Breton."

Sir Walter Raleigh, who had now become possessor of the patent to the discovery of the Cabots, on the death of Sir Humphrey, named the country Virginia; named, as Sir Ferdinando Gorges says, "in memory and honor of the Virgin Queen the wonder of her sex."

Raleigh did not push his enterprises to the northern parts. He, however, sent Mace to rescue his colonists of Virginia. On Mace's return in 1602 Raleigh went to Weymouth (England) to confer with him. Here he found to his amazement Capt. Bartholomew Gosnold, who had just returned from a voyage to Norumbega, made without his permission, and whose little bark called *Concord*, of Dartmouth, was unloading the fragrant cedar and sassafras he had obtained. This voyage is exceedingly interesting as Gosnold's description of the country has been fully preserved. It does not, however, add anything to the history of Monhegan but bolsters up the idea that Maine and Massachusetts were the "Drogeo" of the Zeni chart, because of their herbs and drugs.

Raleigh confiscated Gosnold's cargo on the grounds that the voyage was made without his consent and therefore contraband. Gosnold turned diplomatic and finally appeased Raleigh who shortly became rather pleased with the turn of affairs and resolved to send out both ships again. Gosnold is believed to have discovered the short northern route on this trip.

Queen Elizabeth died in 1603 and as ever the case with favorites, Raleigh's career soon came to an end. However, two voyages were sent out to Virginia under his authority during 1603. One was under Gilbert in the *Elizabeth* to South Virginia, the other to North Virginia and conducted by Martin Pring, with two small vessels, the *Speedwell* and the *Discoverer*. This expedition was financed by Hakluyt and the chief merchants of Bristol, of whom Robert Aldsworth was the "chief furtherer as well with his purse as with his trauell."

Pring sighted land in 43½ N. L. and undoubtedly he dropped anchor in Monhegan's harbor shortly after, and his crew refreshed themselves on the island, for he says:

"We sayled to the southwest end of these Islands (43 degrees of latitude) and there rode with out ships under one of the greatest."

His trip to the southward and the freighting of his boats with sassafras, the drug so much esteemed at that time, is exceedingly interesting to the history of New England.

During these years that the English were exploring

Maine's shore line the French were also visiting the shores of Norumbega. In 1604 De Monts and Champlain established themselves at St. Croix.

SKETCH BY WILLIAM CAMDEN CLARENCIEUX, HERALD, OF PERSONS IN THE FUNERAL PROCESSION OF ELIZABETH, QUEEN OF ENGLAND

Taken from a roll twenty-eight feet long in British Museum. Important personages having their names written over them. (From *Fortescue Family,* New York Public Library. Popham is the first figure to the left.)

CHAPTER VIII

THE Waymouth voyage, sent out by Thomas Arundell, Baron of Wardour, a son-in-law of the Earl of Southampton, was the important voyage of 1605, in the annals of Monhegan. Rosier, the historian of the enterprise, gives a glowing account of the island. This states that:

"But the commodities and profits of the countrey, together with the fitnesse of plantation, being by some honorable Gentlemen of good woorth and qualitie, and Merchants[28] of good sufficiency and judgment duly considered, haue at their owne charge (intending both their priuate and the common benefit of their Country) vndertaken the transporting of a Colony for the plantation thereof:[29] being encouraged thereunto by the gracious fauour of the KING'S MAJESTY himselfe, and diuers Lords of his Highnesse most Honorable Priuie Councell. After these purposed designs were concluded, I was animated to publish this briefe Relation and not before because some forrein Nations (being fully assured of the fruitfulnesse of the countrie) haue hoped thereby to gaine some knowledge of the place, seeing they could not allure our Captaine or any special man of our Company to combine with them for their direction nor obtaine their purposes,

[28] "East India Fellowship."

[29] Prominent among them were Sir Ferdinando Gorges and Sir John Popham, Lord Chief Justice of England.

in conveying away our Saluages, which was busily in practice. And this is the cause that I haue neither written of the latitude or variation most exactly observed by our Captaine with sundrie instruments, which together with his perfect Geographical Map of the countrey, he intendeth hereafter to set forth."

He continues his preamble, stating that he also withholds a collection of four hundred words in the Indian language.

This expedition set sail, supposedly in the *Archangel*, from Ratcliffe, on the 5th of March, but on account of contrary winds did not get under way until the end of the month. They found their sea charts very faulty, but after many tribulations they sighted land.

"Friday the 17th of May about sixe a clocke at night we descried the land, which bare from vs North-Northeast; but because it blew a great gale of winde, the sea very high and neere night, not fit to come vpon an vnknowen coast, we stood off till two a clocke in the morning, being Saturday: then standing in with it againe, we descried it by eight a clocke in the morning, bearing North-East from us. It appeared a meane high land, as we after found it, being but an Iland of some sixe miles in compasse, but I do hope the most fortunate euer yet discoured. About twelve a clocke that day, we came to an anchor on the North side of this Iland, about a league from shore. About two a clocke our Captaine with twelue men rowed in his ship boat to the shore, where we made no long stay, but laded our boat with dry wood of olde trees vpon the shore side and returned to our ship, where we rode that night.

"This iland is woody, grouen with Firre, Birch, Oke and Beech, as farre as we saw along the shore; and so likely to be within. On the verge grow Gooseberries, Strawberries, Wild pease and Wild rose bushes. The water issued forth down the Rocky cliffes in many places: and much fowle of diuers kind breed vpon the shore and rocks.

"While we were at shore, our men aboard with a few hooks got above thirty great Cods and Haddocks, which gaue vs a taste of the great plenty of fish which we found afterward wheresoeuer we went vpon the coast.

"From hence we might descerne the maine land from the West-South-West to the East-North-East, and a great way (as it then seemed, and as we afterward found it) vp into the Maine we might duscerne very high mountaines (Camden Hills), though the maine seemed but low land: which gaue vs a hope it would please God to direct vs to the discouerie of some good; although wee were driuen by winds farre from the place, whither (both by our direction and desire) we euer intended to shape the course of our voyage.

"The next day being Whit-Sunday, because we rode too much open to the sea and windes, we weyed anker about twelue a clocke, and came along to the other Ilands more adjoyning to the maine, and in the rode directly with the mountaines, about three leagues from the first Iland where we had ankered."[30]

Throughout the whole *Relation* of Rosier the distances are overestimated and historians, taking as gospel every statement, have been much misled by this narrative as they have been by others of the same period. Most voyagers for discovery were instructed to guard their discoveries from knowledge of the other nations.

"To prevent the interference of other nations, it was the policy of Weymouth and his patrons not to disclose the locality of the region he explored; and consequently Rosier, the narrator of the voyage, so skillfully withheld whatever might clearly identify the place, and couched his descriptions in such indefinite language, that there has been and is now a great diversity of opinion among local historians."[31]

Waymouth named Monhegan St. George, and it is probable that he put up the cross that the Popham Colony found. Rosier admits to withholding information likely to be of help to "forrein Nations." Waymouth might possibly have planted the cross on a second visit to the is-

[30] Rosier, *Relation of Waymouth's Voyage, 1605,* Gorges Soc., ed.

[31] *Voyages of Champlain.* Prince ed., p. 92 n.

land when Rosier was not of the company. Or more likely still, the location of the "fortunate Iland" may have been withheld through the request of Sir Ferdinando Gorges and Sir John Popham who intended to send an expedition at once to this island. Some historians have thought that perhaps Pring in his voyage of 1606 may have put the cross on the island, but there can be no question that there was a cross planted on Monhegan when the Popham Colony arrived at the Island they called St. George, as will hereafter be conclusively shown. People had also been here before them for, after Waymouth had found a harbor in the St. George's River, on one of the Georges Islands perhaps, Rosier relates:

"Vpon this Iland, as also vpon the former, we found, (at our first comming to shore) where fire had been made: and about the place were very great egge shelles bigger than goose egges, fish bones, and as we judged the bones of some beast."

It is on this island adjacent that the company found:

". . . great muscels among the rocks; and in some of them many small Pearles; and in one muscell (which we drew up in our net) was found fourteene Pearles, whereof one of pretty bignesse and orient; in another aboue fiftie small Pearles: and if we had had a Drag, no doubt we had found some of great valew, seeing these did certainly shew, that heere they were bred: the shels all glittering with mother of Pearle."

This statement also confirms Ingram's tale of the wonders of Norumbega and the city of Bega.

Rosier's *Relation* is a most interesting tale and should be read by everyone interested in Monhegan's history, but it is too long to be entirely included in this history. One more quotation, however, is necessary:

"The first and chieftest thing required, is a bold coast and faire land to fall with; the next, a safe harbour for ships to ride in.

"The first is a speciall attribute to this shore, being most free from sands or dangerous rocks in a continuall good depth, with a most excellent land fall, which is the first Iland we fell with, *named by vs, Saint Georges Iland.*"[30]

So we have Monhegan named St. Georges Iland by Waymouth. She is designated as a "faire lande fall," and the excellence of her harbor is established in 1605. But the Maine historians insist that it was in Georges River that they captured the five savages that proved so important later. Although Champlain, who was here during the same month and therefore in a better position to know, says that it was from the Kennebec that they were taken, and that the English were at the island of "le Nef," or Monhegan. Their names were:

"1, Tahanado, a Sagamo or Commander; 2, Amoret, his brother; 3, Skicowaros, 4, Maneddo. Gentlemen; 5, Saffacomoit, a seruant."

While Waymouth was still up the Georges River, or the

Penobscot, other illustrious visitors came sailing by on a southerly course. These were Champlain and De Monts, who were searching a more suitable spot for their colonization scheme than St. Croix, where they had wintered, and where the suffering from scurvy had been extreme. They were also seeking the Indian wheat, that the Armouchiquois Indians gathered from the wild plants. They also inquired eagerly for the herb with which the Indians had supplied Cartier, when he had been in this region in 1534 when his crew had been so disastrously depleted with scurvy. But the herb called by Cartier *ameda* was unknown to the Indians of this time, and the older generations were dead.

Champlain's story of his voyages to our locality is here quoted:[32]

"Having made an alliance with them, they guided us to their river of Pentegouet, so called by them, where they told us was their captain, named Bessabez,[33] chief of the river. I think this river is that which several pilots and historians call Norumbegue, and which most have described as large and extensive, with very many islands, its mouth being in latitude 43°, 43′, 30″, according to others in 44°, more or less."

We have in confirmation of Champlain's statement in regard to Norumbega:

"Josephus Acosta in his booke *De Natura noui orbis*

[32] *Voyages of Champlain.* Prince ed., p. 40.

[33] The Bashaba of Ingram, Gorges, and Smith.

indeuors by many reasons to proue, that this part of America was originally inhabited by certaine Indians, forced thither by tempestuous weather ouer the South Sea which now they call *Mare del Zur*. But to me it seems more probable, out of the historie of the two *Zeni*, gentlemen of Venice (which I haue put down before the Fable of the South sea, and before that of Scandia) that this new world many ages past was entered upon by some islanders of *Europe*, as namely of *Greenland, Island*, and *Frisland*; being much neerer thereunto than the Indians, nor distoyned thence (as appears out of the map) by an Ocean so huge, and to the Indians so unnauigable. Also, what also may we coniecture to be signified by this *Norumbega* (the name of a North region of America) but that from Norway, signifying a northland, some colonie in times past hath hither beene transplanted?"[34]

Purchas has this to say of Norumbega:

"A. D. 1607 Contemporaneously with the appearance of a town of fifty houses on the west bank of the Sagadahock at its mouth, defended by a fort, adorned with a church, echoing with the hum and clatter of saws and maul in the hands of busy artisans, on the frame of the *Virginia* of Sagadahock, there was published at Doway, the *Universal History of the West Indies*. This book, of two and a half centuries ago, describes Norumbega, 'as a city toward the north, which is known well enough by

[34] *The Theatre of the Whole World: Set forth by that Excellent Geographer Abraham Ortelius.* London, 1606, p. 5.

reason of a fair town and a great river.' In a further description, it is affirmed, that at the mouth of the river, '*is an island very fit for fishing* . . . and the region that goeth along the sea, doth abound in fish.'"[35]

Monsieur Beauvois has published a theory that the name Norumbegua is no historical myth, but records of a faint tradition of a Scandinavian colony, planted between Markland and Vinland before Columbus sailed. It would seem to have had many believers in it for it to have been even a faint tradition.

"Now from the North
"Of Norumbega and the Samöed shore,
"Bursting their brazen dungeons, armed with ice." MILTON.

If one accepts Ortelius' explanation that Norumbega is a region formerly inhabited by an ancient colony of Norsemen, and what else could it mean? then, locating the island of Monhegan at the entrance of the Penobscot, on the ancient maps, becomes simplified; for this name, Norumbega, is always placed in the region of the Penobscot River. No voyager to that region could have failed to have sighted Monhegan, and as discovery of safe harbors for colonization was one of the aims of the discoverers, it is not rash to assume that all voyagers visited this harbor, which is so comparatively safe from dangerous and hidden rocks.

There is one statement that the earliest account of Norumbega was given by Crigon who is supposed to have

[35] Purchas, *His Pilgrims*, vol. 4, 1620-25.

been in this locality in 1539. This your author has not been able to verify.

A list of some of the various forms of the spelling of the word may be useful: Aranbega, Rambega, Arembec, Anorabaga, Verrazano material; Anorombega, Americus Vespucia; Nurumbega, Parmentier, Mercator, Magin, Wytfliet; La Norumbega, Wytfliet; Norobega, Magin; Norombega, Ortelius; Norombegue, Alphonse; Norambegue, Thevet and Biard; Norembegue, Noremberga, Noranberga, Champlain; Norembegue, I de Vaulx; Norumberg, editions of Ptolémée of 1548, 1561; Norovagia, Mappe Monde of Henry II; Norumbegia, Hakluyt; Norombegue, Beauvois; Norbegia Regnum, Waldseemüller. The modern Spanish word for Norwegians is Noruego.

There are many more instances of the spelling of the name, but these are enough to satisfy. As late as 1663 the map makers were still putting this name on the regions near the Penobscot, although in the *Les Relations des Jesuites*, 1611-16,[36] there is a statement regarding the word that is interesting:

"Acadie, or the Souriquoys country, further south is next to Canada, and still further down, on the other side of French Bay, is Norombegue. Of these two words, Norombegue and Acadie, there no longer remains any remembrance in the country."

Champlain probably put in to Monhegan's harbor on September 20, 1604, as he says:

[36] *Les Relations des Jesuites*, vol. 3, p. 41.

"We sailed some eight leagues along the Western coast to an island, ten leagues distance from Quinibeguy, where we were obliged to put in on account of bad weather and contrary winds."

On his voyage of 1605 he says of Monhegan:

"On Friday the 1st of July, we set out from one of the islands at the mouth of the river, where there is a very good harbor for vessels of a hundred or 150 tons."

While these French voyagers were tarrying at the Kennebec River harbor, his account continues:

"From here large mountains are seen to the west, in which is the dwelling place of a savage captain called Aneda, who encamps near this river Quinibeguy. I was satisfied that it was one of his tribe that had discovered the plant called Aneda, which Jacques Cartier said was so powerful against the malady called scurvy. . . . The Savages had no knowledge of this plant.

"While waiting there came to us a captain called Anasson, who trafficked a little in furs, and with whom we had made an alliance. He told us that there was a ship ten leagues off the harbour,[37] which was engaged in fishing, and that those on her had killed five savages of this river, under cover of friendship. From his description of the men on the vessel, we concluded that they were English, and we named the island where they were La Nef; for, at a distance, it had the appearance of a ship."

In this account he places the capturers of the Indians

[37] *Sieur Champlain's Voyages.* Prince ed.

at La Nef, 10 leagues from the Kennebec, and as this is the distance he mentioned of "an island" in his former voyage of 1604 it definitely settles the fact that he twice visited Monhegan's harbor. All historians agree that Monhegan was La Nef. It might be well to mention here that "Old Membertou," who saw Jacques Cartier, and was even married and had children at that time, was still living when these Frenchmen came later.

But the Indians had not been killed but had been taken to England, and three of them falling into the hands of Sir Ferdinando Gorges had been very kindly dealt with as his account will show.

The naming of Monhegan "La Nef" by Champlain is the second christening of the island within a month's time; "St. George," by the Englishman Waymouth, and "La Nef," by the Frenchman Champlain.

Many circumstances found in the *Champlain Voyages* lead to the inevitable conclusion that this was indeed Vinland the Good, or Markland.

Champlain and De Monts found an island, which they named "Bacchus," in the Kennebec, because there they found excellent vines growing wild that produced grapes in their season. They were searching for the wild wheat, that the Archimoquois Indians gathered, to relieve their scanty provisions. We know now that the *masur* wood, of the country of Vinland the Good, may have been the boles of the birch trees, or the bird's-eye maple, which abound everywhere.

These items are the ones local historians have used for the identification of those legendary countries, and they are all found in this region. Then this name Norumbega, spelled in dozens of different ways, has always led to the region of the Penobscot. As to the significance of the word

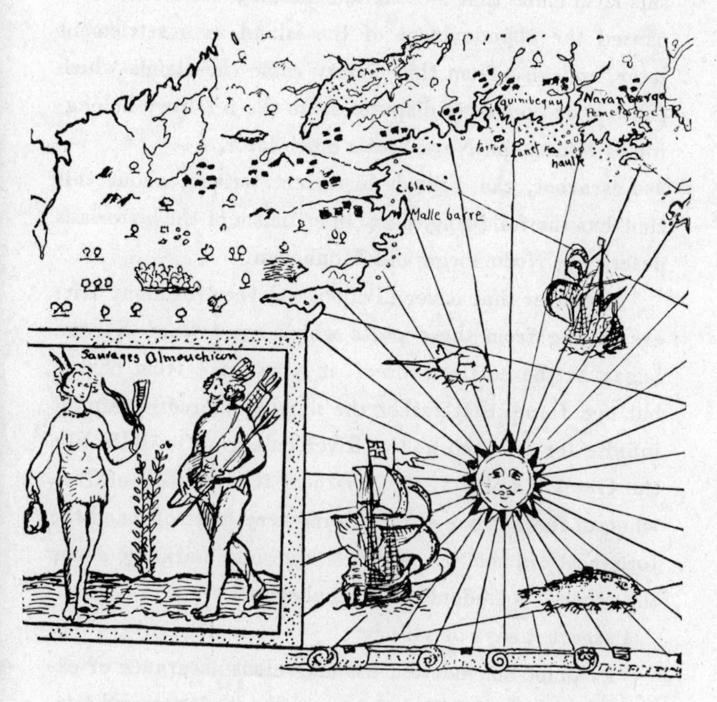

PORTION OF CHAMPLAIN'S MAP SHOWING MONHEGAN AS LA NEF

Traced from original map in *Voyages de Sieur de Champlain*, Paris, 1613, in New York Public Library

there can be scarcely a doubt that it meant Norse settlement or land of the Norse.

The early history of the settlements and claims of the French to this territory under the discovery of Verrazano is important, in the history of Monhegan, as it was from this rival claim that the terrible Indian Wars arose which caused the abandonment of the island as a settlement later, and also from this rivalry came the claims which caused the boundary disputes as to the territory belonging to Maine and Nova Scotia much later.

Lescarbot, the French historian, writing about this time has the following to say in criticism of the historians describing Norumbega and Monhegan.

"Moreover that River (Penobscot) receives many Rivers falling from those parts which are toward Norombega: At the entrie whereof, it is so farre from having but one Iland, that rather the number thereof is almost infinite for as much as the River enlarging its selfe like the Greek Lamba Λ, the mouth of it is all full of Iles, whereof there is one of them lying very farre off (and the fore most) in the Sea, which is high and markable above the others." (Undoubtedly Monhegan.)

Lescarbot says of sailors:

"I cannot but mention the marvelous assurance of experienced sailors during these squalls, cyclones, and tempests. With the boat traveling up mountains of water and then sliding to the depths of profound abysses, they climb the ropes, not only to the maintop, but without footholds, to the other masts branching out from it, holding themselves only by the strength of their arms and their feet twisted around the ropes. Moreover, if during a storm the mainsail (which they call Paphil or Papefust) rips loose from the top, the first man commanded to do so puts himself astraddle the main yard and with a hammer at his belt and half a dozen nails in his mouth, risking a thousand perils, fastens the loosened sail to its place."

CHAPTER IX

THE story of the first vigorous enterprises of the English of the North Virginia Colony should now be told by Sir Ferdinando Gorges who, in his *Abriefe Relation of the Discovery* and *Plantation of New England,* and *Briefe Narration,* gives the real and best accounts that have come down to us.[38]

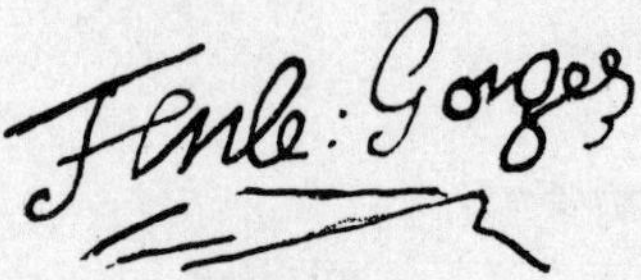

"And so it pleased our great God that ther hapned to come into the harbour of *Plymouth* (where I then commanded) one Captain *Waymouth* that had been imployed by the Lord *Arundell* of *Warder* for the discovery of the North-west passage.

"But falling short of his Course, hapned into a River on the Coast of *America,* called *Pemmaquid,* from whence he brought five of the Natives, three of whose names were *Manida, Skettwarroes,* and *Tasquantum,* whom I seized upon; they were all of one Nation, but of severall parts, and severall Families; This accident must be acknowledges the means under God of putting on foote, and giv-

[38] *Gorges and His Province of Maine,* Prince ed., 3 vols.

ing life to all our Plantations, as by the ensuing discourse will manifestly appears.

"After I had those people sometimes in my Custody, I observed in them an inclination to follow the example of the better sort; And in all their carrigges manifest shewes of great civility farre from the rudenesse of our common people; And the longer I conversed with them, the better hope they gave me of those parts where they did inhabit, as proper for our uses, especially when I found what goodly Rivers, stately Islands, and safe Harbours those parts abounded with, being the speciall marks I levelled at as the onely want our Nation met with in all their Navigations along that Coast, and haveing kept them full three yeares, I made them able to set me downe what great Rivers ran up into the Land, what Men of note were seated on them, what power they were of, how allyed, what enemies they had, and the like of which in his proper place.

"Those credible informations the Natives had given me of the condition and state of their Country, made me send away a Ship (*Richard of Plymouth*) furnished with Men and all necessaries, provisions convenient for the service intended, under command of Captain *Henry Challoung*, a gentleman of good Fâmily, industrious, and of fair condition, to whom I gave such directions and instructions for his better direction as I knew proper for his use, and my satisfaction, being grounded upon the information I had of the Natives, sending two of them with him to aver the same, Binding both the Captain his Master, and company strictly to follow it; or to expect the miscarriage of the Voyage to be laid unto their Charge, Commanding them by all meanes to keep the northerly gage, as high as Cape Britton, till they had discovered the Maine, and then to beat it up to the Southward, as the Coast tended, till they found by the Natives they were neer the place they were assigned unto; Though this were a direction contrary to the opinion of our best Sea-men of these times; yet I knew many reasons persuading me thereunto, as well as for that I understood the Natives themselfes to be exact Pilots for that Coast, having been accustomed to frequent the same, both as Fishermen and in passing along the shoare to seek their enemies, that dwelt to the Northward of them; But it is not in the wit of Man to prevent the providence of the most High.

"For this Captain being some 100 leagues of the Island of Canara, fell sick of a Feaver, and the winds being Westerly, his company shaped their course for the *Indies*, and coming to *St. John de Porteriko*, the Captain himselfe went a shoare for the recovery of his health, whiles the Company took in water, and such other provision as they had present us of, expending some time there, hunting after such things as best pleased themselves; That ended, they set their course to fall with their owne height they were directed unto; By which meanes they met the *Spanish* Fleet that came from *Havana*, by whom they were taken and carried into *Spaine*, where their Ship and goods were confiscate, themselves made Prisoners, the voyage overthrowne, and both my Natives lost; This the gaine of their breach of Order, which afterward observed, brought all our Shippes to their desired Ports; The affliction of the Captain and his Company put the Lord Chief Justice *Popham* to charge, and myselfe to trouble in procuring their liberties, which was not suddenly obtained.

"Shortly upon my sending away of Captaine *Challounge*, it pleased the Lord Chief Justice according to his promise to dispatch Captain *Prin* from *Bristoll*, with hope to have found Captaine *Challounge*, where by his instructions he was assigned, who observing the same, happily arrived there, but not hearing by any means what had become of him, (Challounge) after he had made a perfect discovery of all those Rivers and Harbours he was informed of by his instructions, (the season of the year requiring his return) brings with him the most exact discovery of that Coast thatever came to my hands since, and indeed he was the best able to performe it of any I met withall to this present, which with the relation of the Country, wrought such an impression in the Lord Chief

Justice, and us all that were his associates, that (notwithstanding our first disaster) we set up our resolutions to follow it with effect, and that upon better grounds, for as yet, our authority was but in motion."

Brown, in his *Genesis of the United States*, says:

"Hanham and Pring, who sailed for North Virginia in October 1606, returned to England early in 1607, possibly in April. Hanham's Relation was in the hands of the Rev. Samuel Purchas, in 1624, but the accounts are now lost. Pring's 'exact discovery' also seems not accessible."[39]

Analyzing this statement of Gorges it would appear that Pring was the cartographer and the Relation was by another hand. The statement of Brown, therefore, that Hanham went on this voyage and wrote a Relation may clarify the subject. It is barely possible that the "Simancas Map" may have been the Pring "exact discovery" that Sir Ferdinando means.

This was the third voyage for Pring and he undoubtedly sailed for Waymouth's Ile. St. George, as he knew the country well. His may have been the hand that put up the cross that was found later, but from various aspects of the case it would appear that the cross was erected by Waymouth. The return of Pring with his "exact discovery," added to the news brought the year before by Waymouth, must have fired these zealous colonizers to a great pitch of excitement.

[39] Brown, *Genesis of the United States*, vol. 1, p. 99.

Where the cross stood is subject for conjecture. School House Hill seems to offer the best site, as from that position it could easily have been seen by passing craft. In any other position, near the little beaches, it would have been concealed by Manana.

It is evident, from Gorges story, that soon after Waymouth's return the Lord Chief Justice Popham launched the scheme for the granting of a Royal Charter for Virginia. According to this charter granted by King James in 1606, Virginia, while being under one governing Council, was to be divided into two colonies:

". . . the first (South Virginia Colony) undertaken by Nobel Men, Knights, Gentlemen and Merchants in and about the City of London, the second (North Virginia Colony) by certaine Knights, Gentlemen, and Merchants in the western parts."[40]

The Spanish during this period were still keeping a watchful eye on the English activities in the North American continent, for we have a letter from Don Pedro de Zũniga written to the King of Spain in 1607, which after exhorting the King of Spain to take measures against the English as he thought that they were establishing a nest for pirates, says:

"I have found a confidential person, through whom, I shall find out what shall be in the Council (which they call the Council of Virginia). They are in a great state of

[40] Gorges, *Briefe Narration. Gorges and His Province of Maine.* Prince ed., vol. 2, p. 12.

excitement about that place, and very much afraid lest your Majesty should drive them out of it."[41]

Evidently there was a traitor in the English camp of either Catholic or Spanish sympathies, as the meetings of the Council were private and the members sworn to secrecy. A hint has been thrown out that possibly the furtherer of the Waymouth voyage, Sir Thomas Arundell of Wardour, or his father-in-law, the Earl of Southampton, who were both strong Catholics, may have been the guilty ones.

Another letter from Zũniga, dated October 5, 1607, tells the Spanish King that the English are complaining that King James does too much for the Scotch, "that he favors them more than themselves."

Perhaps it might be well to explain here the relationship existing between these early adventurers.

Sir Ferdinando Gorges was a cousin, through the Champernowne family, to Sir Humphrey Gilbert, Adrian Gilbert, Sir John Gilbert, Sir Walter Raleigh and also to Sir Humphrey's son, Raleigh Gilbert. The first "seizin," as Sir Ferdinando calls it, the exploration and development of the North American continent is, therefore, principally due to the enterprise of this family. Hakluyt gives the tales of many of these voyages.

Sir Ferdinando seems to have made a good impression on Sir John Popham, Lord Chief Justice of England. Possibly the friendship that existed between them had its

[41] Brown, *Genesis of the United States.*

SEAL OF THE COUNCIL OF VIRGINIA, "HIS MAJESTIES COUNCIL OF VIRGINIA." THE SEAL OF THE COUNCIL OF THE NORTH VIRGINIA OR SECOND COLONY WAS EXACTLY LIKE THE ABOVE, SAVE IN PLACE OF "PRO CONCILIO SUO VIRGINIAE," THERE WERE THE WORDS "PRO CONCILIO SECUNDAE COLONIAE VIRGINIAE"

From Brown's *Genesis of the United States*, vol. I, p. 57

origin at the time, in 1600, when Essex, plotting against the Queen, captured and held prisoners the Lord Chief Justice Popham, along with the Lord Keeper, Egerton, the Controller of the Queen's Household, Knollys, and the Earl of Worcester. Gorges, although a friend of Essex, liberated them. Also the Lord Chief Justice's daughter, Elizabeth, married into the Champernowne family.

The twenty-year war between England and Spain ended in 1606 and it is evident that Sir John Popham and Sir Ferdinando Gorges decided that with the Spanish treaty it was now safe to start colonization plans. The English public men at this time were all writing about Plantations and how they should be established. Bacon wrote a treatise which undoubtedly influenced the policies followed by Gorges and Popham. It is quite evident that it was thought unwise to plant, as they called it, with women until the colony was in a condition to receive them.

This colonization scheme of the Popham Colony was probably too hastily gotten together, but at any rate, on May 31, 1607, two ships, the *Gift of God,* commanded by George Popham, an elderly relative of Sir John Popham's, and the *Mary and John,* Raleigh Gilbert commanding, set sail for the "Ile of St. Georges."

Of the voyage of the *Mary and John* we have a full account written by J. Davis. This manuscript, *Relations of a Voyage to Sagadahoc,* was encountered by the Reverend Benjamin Franklin DeCosta, when searching for other material, in the Lambeth Palace Library, in 1875, which he published in 1880.

The *Mary and John,* in which evidently the narrator, J. Davis, was master, barely escaped being captured by the Netherlanders as the Dutch were called. DeCosta, who made a very careful and unbiased study of the trip, gives an outline of the sailing course as follows:

"Finally leaving the Azores, Gilbert stood to sea, crossing the ocean alone, and sighted the hills of Le Havre, Nova Scotia, July 30. After visiting the harbor of Le Havre, Gilbert sailed southward rounding Cape Sable, and entered the 'great deep Bay of Fundy.'

"He then passed the seal islands, evidently being well acquainted with the ground, and next shaped his course for the region of the Penobscot, looking in the meantime for the Camden Hills, which on the afternoon of Aug. 5 lifted their double peaks above the bright summer sea. He confidently stood in toward the land, the Matinicus Islands soon shone white 'like unto Dover Cliffs'; and afterward the *Mary and John* found good anchorage close under Monhegan, Waymouth's fortunate island, named in honor of England's patron saint, St. George. Landing upon the island Gilbert found a sightly cross, which had been set up by Waymouth or some other navigator."

We will now quote Davis' words in regard to the landing and Thanksgiving Service which has caused some discontent to the Boston historians.

RELATION OF A VOYAGE TO SAGADAHOC

From hence we kept still our Course West and West by North toward three other Islands that we Sawe Lyenge from these Illands beffor spoken of 8 Leags and about ten of the Cloke att nyght we recovered them and havinge Sent in our bott beffor nyght to vew ytt for that ytt was Calme a(nd) to Sound ytt and See whatt good ankoringe was under ytt we bot in wth on (one) of them the wch as we cam in by we still sounded and founde very deep watt^{r} 40 fetham hard abord of yt. So we stood in into a Cove In ytt and had 12 fetham watt^{r} and thear we ankored untill the mornynge. And when the daye appeared We Saw we weare environed Round about with Illands. yo myght have told neare thirty Illands round about us from abord our shipe. this Illand we Call S^{t}. Georges Illand for that we hear found a Crosse Sett up the wch we Suppose was Sett up by George Wayman.

Frydaye beinge the 7th of Auguste we wayed our Ankor whereby to bringe our shipe in mor bett^{r} Safty how Soever the wynd should happen to blow and about ten of the Cloke in the mornynge as we weare standinge of a Lyttell from the Illand we descried a saill standinge in towards this Illand and we presently mad towards her and found ytt to be the GYFTE our Consort So beinge all Joye full of our happy meetinge we both stood in again for the Illand we ryd under beffor and theare ankored both to gether.

This night folloyinge about mydnyght Capt. Gilbert caussed his ships bott to be manned and took to himselfe 13 other my Selffe beinge on (e), beinge 14 persons in all, and tooke the Indian Skidwarres wth us the weather beinge fairr and the wynd Calme we rowed to the Weste in amongst many gallant Illands and found the ryver of pemaquid to be but 4 Leags weste from the Illand we call S^{t}. Georges whear our ships remained at Anckor. hear we landed in a Lyttell Cove by skyd warres Direction and marched over a necke of the Land near three mills. so the Indian skidwarres brought us to the Salvages housses whear they did inhabitt although much against his will for that he told us that they wear all removed and gon from the place they wear wont to inhabitt. but we answered hem again that we wold nott retorn backe untill shutch time as we had spoken with Som of them. At Length he brought us whear they did inhabytt whear we found near a hundredth of them men wemen and Children. And the Cheeff Commander of them ys Nahanada. att our fryste Seight of them uppon a howlinge or Cry that they mad they all presently Isued forth towards us wth thear bowes and arrows and we presently mad a stand and Suffered them to Com near unto us. then our Indian skidwarres spoke unto them in thear language showinge them that we wear wch when Nahanada thear Comander perseaved what we wear he Caussed them all to laye assyd thear bowes and arrowes and cam unto us and imbrassed us and we did the lyke to them aggain. So we remained wth them near to howers and wear in thear housses. Then we tooke our Leave of them and retorned wth our Indyan Skidwarres wth us towards our ships the 8 Daye of August being Satterdaye in the after noon.

Sondaye being the 9th of Auguste in the morninge the most p^{t} of our holl company of both our shipes Landed on this Illand the wch we call S^{t}. Georges Illand whear the Crosse standeth and thear we heard a Sermon delyvred unto us by our preacher (Rev. Richard Seymour) gyvinge god thanks for our happy metinge and Saffe aryvall into the Contry and So retorned abord aggain.

DeCosta, who is perhaps the most important historian of this period of American history, says:

"This, so far as our present information extends, is the first recorded religious service by any English or Protestant clergyman within the bounds of New England, which was then consecrated to christian civilization."

The Journal of Davis continues:

Mundaye beinge the Xth of Auguste early in the morninge Capt popham in his shallope wth thirty others and Capt Gilbert in his ships bott wth twenty others Acompanede Depted from thear shipes and sailled towards the ryver of pemaquyd and caryed wth us the Indyan skidwarres and Cam to the ryver ryght beffore thear housses whear they no Sooner espyed us but presently Nahanada wth all his Indyans wth thear bowes and arrows in thear hands Cam forth upon the Sands. So we Caussed skidwarres to speak unto hem and we our Selves spok unto hem in Inglyshe givinge hem to understand our Comenge tended to no yvell towards hem Selffe nor any of his peopell. he told us again he wold nott thatt all our peopell should Land. So because we would in no sort offend them, hearuppon Som ten or twelffe of the Cheeff gent Landed and had Some parle together and then afterward they wear well contented that all should Land. So we all landed we ussinge them wth all the kindnesse that possibell we Could. neverthelesse after an hower or to thev all Soddainly withdrew them Selves from us into the woods and Lefte us. we perseavinge this presently imbarked our Selves all except Skid warres who was not Desjerous to retorn with us. we Seeinge this woold in no Sort proffer any Violence unto hem by drawing hem perforce Suffered hem to remain, and staye behinde us, he promyssinge to retorn unto us the next Daye followinge but he heald not his promysse. So we imbarked our Selves and went unto the other syd of the ryver and thear remained uppon the shore the nyght followinge.

Tuesdaye beinge the Xi[th] of Auguste we retorned and cam to our ships whear they still remained att ankor under the Illand we call S[t] Georges.

Wensdaye being the Xii[th] of Auguste we wayed our anckors and Sett our saills to go for the ryver of Sagadehock. we kept our Course from thence dew Weste until 12 of the clok mydnyght of the Sam. then we stroke our

Saills and layed a hull untill the mornynge Doutinge for to over shoot ytt.

This account was probably written for Gorges, as it was found among his papers by "me William Griffith."

The passengers known to have been on the *Gift of God* and the *Mary and John* were:[42]

Capt. George Popham, President of the Second Colony of Virginia and Senior in command; Raleigh Gilbert, Admiral; Edward Harlow, Master of Ordnance; Robert Dauis, Sergeant at Arms—major commander; Ellis Best, Marshal; John Scammon, Secretary of Colony; Mr. Turner, Physician;[43] Gome Carew, Searcher; Richard Seymour, a Champernowne, Minister; Henry Harley;[43] Shetwarrowes, Dehameda, Savages.

Capt. George Popham, president of the Second Colony of Virginia, and senior in command, is described by Gorges in one of his letters[44] to the Earl of Salisbury, December 3, 1607, as well as Captain Gilbert, as follows:

"For firste the President himselfe is an honest man, but ould, and of an unwildy body, and timerously fearfull to offende or contest wth others that will or do oppose him, but otherwise a discreete carefull man. Captayne Gilberte[45] is described to mee from thence to bee disirous of

[42] Williamson, *History of Maine.* [43] Gorges.

[44] *Gorges and His Province of Maine.* Prince ed., vol. 3, pp. 158, 159.

[45] Raleigh Gilbert was the son of Sir Humphrey Gilbert, whose title had been assigned by him to Sir Thomas Gerrard and Sir George Peckham.

supremasy, and rule, a loose life, prompt to sensuality, litle zeale in Religion, humerouse, head stronge, and of small judgment and experiense, other wayes valiant inough, but hee houldes that the kinge could not give away that, by Pattent, to others, wch his Father had an Act of Parliament for, and that hee will not bee put out of it in haste, wth many such like idle speeches, w^ch^ (allthough hee bee powerlesse to performe oughte) weare not unfit to bee taken notice of bycause it weare good in my opinion that all such occasion were taken away, as may hinder the publique proceedinge, and let the cause of sedition bee plucked up by the Roote, before it do more harme; besides hee hath sent (as I am farther informed) into England for divers of his friendes, to com to him, for the strenghning of his party on all occasions (as hee termes it) wth much more that I have receaved notis of to this effect."

The errors of historians[46] regarding the landing of the Popham Colony on Monhegan can be easily understood as they did not have in the earlier times the Davis account of the voyage of the *Mary and John*.

In 1899, or thereabout, Alexander Brown, while gathering material for the study of the South Virginia Colony, *The Genesis of the United States*, discovered a map

[46] The controversy regarding the Popham colony was heated and extensive, and continued for many years. A summary of the contestants and their views will be found in the Bulletin VIII, 1875-1878, Boston Public Library. A better summing up of the matter is found in *Gorges and His Province of Maine*. Prince ed., vol. 1, p. 86, n. 126.

MARY AND JOHN AND THE GYFTE IN MONHEGAN HARBOR, AUG. 5, 1607
From Rufus King Sewall's *Ancient Voyages to the Western Continent*

in the Royal Library of Spain at Simancas which places the Ile St. George in Monhegan's position, and at last clears up this disputed question beyond any uncertainty. Brown says of the map:

"This map, said to have been made in Virginia by a surveyor sent over by the King of England for that purpose, who returned to England about December, 1610, procured in some secret way by the Spanish Ambassador

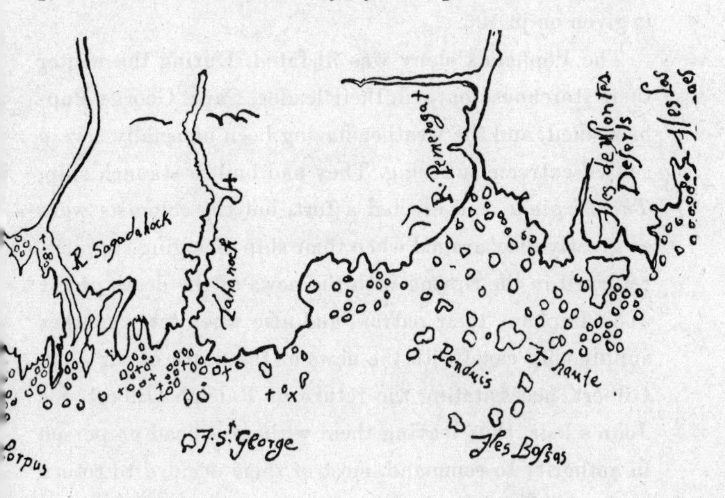

PORTION OF SIMANCAS MAP, 1610, SHOWING LOCATION OF ILE ST. GEORGE
From Brown's *Genesis of the United States*

in London and sent to the King of Spain is very interesting and valuable. . . .

"I think the map evidently embodies (besides the surveys of Champlain and other foreigners) the English surveys of White, Gosnold, Weymouth, Pring, Hudson, Argall, and Tyndall, and possibly others."

The portion of this, "The Simancas Map," which shows part of North Virginia and the location of Ile St. George is given on p. 105.

The Popham Colony was ill-fated. During the winter their storehouse burned, their leader, Capt. George Popham, died, and the weather having been unusually severe caused extreme suffering. They had built a staunch ship, *The Virginia,* and erected a fort, but the colonists were so greatly discouraged when their ship, bringing supplies, returned in the Spring with the news of the death of Sir John Popham, their patron, and also when later another supply ship came with the news of the death of Sir John Gilbert, necessitating the return of Raleigh Gilbert, Sir John's heir, thus leaving them without a head or person in authority to command, most of them decided to return to England. Gorges had written to the Earl of Salisbury on December 3, 1607, that something should be done about the factions in the colony, and recommended the physician, Mr. Turner, or Captain Davis.[47]

It is from the account of Harlow that we learn that forty-five of the colony did not return to England.[47] What

[47] Sylvester, *Pioneer Settlements of Maine, Monhegan.*

became of them is not now known. Evidently they did not stay at the fort or the French when they visited it so soon afterward would have found some sign of them, which from their rather full account is not noted. It may be that they built themselves a fishing boat and remained in the vicinity, or returned to Monhegan where they would be in more safety and where Gorges was about to establish his fishing station, then later going back to New Harbor. Nothing seems to be known of their fate, excepting for legends, to this day. Sullivan in his history says:

"That it is a tradition of his lifetime that there were people at Pemaquid who did not venture far away from their settlement." They may have stayed with some of the friendly Sagamores of the Bashaba. It is evident from Gorges' account that at least one ship had returned to England before Popham's death, as he says: "Captayne Gilbert is described to me from thence." Undoubtedly he sent a ship to Monhegan at once, in 1608, and possibly before Gilbert's return and before Vines was sent, which was in 1609. This would solve the question of what happened to the forty-five who remained.

Sir Ferdinando Gorges, although greatly discouraged, as he says, reasoned, as we find in his *Brief Narration*, that the cold was unusual even in England that winter and that many countries further north were inhabited, he says:[48]

"Finding I could no longer be seconded by others, I

[48] *Gorges and His Province of Maine.* Prince ed., vol. 2, p. 18.

became owner of a Ship myselfe, fit for that imployment, and under colour of fishing and trade, I got a Master and company for her, to which I sent *Vines* and others my owne servants with their provisions for trade and discovery, appointing them to leave the Ship and Ships company for to follow their businesse in the usual place, (for I knew they would not be drawn to seek by any meanes) by these and the help of those natives formerly sent over, I came to be truly informed of so much as gave me assurance that in time I should want no undertakers, though as yet I was forced to hire Men to stay there the Winter Quarter at extreame rates, and not without danger, for that the War had consumed the Bashaba, and the most of those great Sagamores, with such Men of action as followed them, and those that remained were sore afflicted with the Plague, for that the Country was in a manner left void of Inhabitants." ". . . and this course I held for some years together . . ."

From this account, which is indeed brief, it would appear that Sir Ferdinando sent, during the season of 1608, a ship for fishing and trade, but that he was disappointed in their efforts at discovery. Vines was in America in 1609,[49] "several years before any other inhabitant could be found," and he was instructed to leave the ship in the "usuall place" (Monhegan) where they remained during the winter quarter, "at extreme rates and not without

[49] *Gorges and His Province of Maine.* Prince ed., vol. 1, p. 132, n. 177.

danger," because of the death of the friendly chiefs. It would seem that the date of the occupation of Monhegan as a settled fishing station or plantation began in 1608.

Sullivan says of Monhegan, that Gorges made a settlement there in 1616; but undoubtedly it was made before that, or in 1608 or 9.

The failure of the Popham Colony caused the South Virginia Colony to put in a bid for colonization of the North Virginia territory, but without avail. The ship *Virginia*, however, went with them in the colonization voyage to Jamestown in 1609.

CHAPTER X

HAVING established Monhegan as the fishing plantation of Gorges and the Second Colony of Virginia, sometimes called the Plymouth Company, we will now relate the visitors who happened to call.

Henry Hudson is credited with having dropped his anchor in Monhegan's harbor in 1609, while in the next year came Captain Argall, from the South Virginia Colony, in search for supplies. Where else, than at Gorges' fishing station, could he expect to get supplies?

Sir Francis Popham, heir of Sir John, according to Gorges, *Brief Relation*, continued sending ships for fishing and trade to the region of the former location of the Popham Colony for several years. One of Sir Francis' captains, Captain Williams, was fishing in these waters during the seasons of 1610,[50] 1611 and 1612. We also know from Capt. John Smith that Sir Francis was sending his ships in 1614.

We have Sylvester's word[51] for the fact that Monhegan was called E. mmetinic at this period:

"In these days, it may be well to mention, that this island had another name. It was often designated E. mmetinic when the fishing stages were first set up here;

[50] Bolton, *Real Founders of New England*, p. 170.
[51] Sylvester, *Maine Pioneer Settlements, Monhegan.*

as Monhegan, and by which name the island was more anciently known. The origin as well as the derivation of E. mmetinic is obscure but the name has come down, and one meets it, here and there, as some annalist of the seventeenth century assays to locate some episode of those early years which had its setting in the neighborhood, or about the neighboring waters."

The only record found by your author, in which this name is given to an island in this locality, is in an account of Father Pierre Biard to the Right Reverend Provincial at Paris, preserved in the archives of Jesus at Rome, dated January 31, 1612, Port Royal, which I give in full, as it reflects the French attitude of the time, and establishes Monhegan as E. mmetinic, "8 leagues from Kennebec."

"I have made two voyages with M. de Biancourt, one lasting nearly twelve days, the other of a month and a half, and we have examined the whole coast from Port Royal as far as Kinibéqui, West-South-West. We have sailed up the large rivers, St. John, the Holy Cross (Saincte Croix), Pentegoet (Penobscot) and the above mentioned Kinibéqui. We have visited the French, who have wintered here this year in two divisions, on the River St. Jean, and that of Sainte Croix; the Malouins (Malecites Indians) at the river St. Jean, and Captain Platrier at Sainte Croix.

"Two main causes induced M. de Biancourt to do this; the first to obtain news about the English and to know if it would be possible to get the better of them; the second to exchange 'Armonchiquoys' wheat so as to preserve us during the winter, and keep us from dying of hunger, in case we should receive no aid from France. In order to understand the first motive, it ought to be known that shortly before Captain Platrier of Honfleur, was taken a prisoner by two English vessels, that were near an island called Emmetenic, 8 leagues from the aforesaid Kinnibéqui. He was released by means of some presents, and the promise he gave to comply with the prohibitions imposed upon him, not to trade along the whole coast. For the English claim to be masters here, and in support of this they exhibit Patents of their King, which we, however, believe to be false. Now M. de Biancourt, having heard all this from the lips of Captain Platrier himself, represented very earnestly to these people how important it was to him, an officer of the Crown and a lieutenant of his father, how important also to every good Frenchman, to go and prevent this usurpation of the English, which was so very contrary to the rights and possessions of his Majesty.

"'For,' said he, 'it is well known to all men (not to speak of higher view of the matter) that the great Henry, who, God may save in his mercy, according to rights acquired by him, and through his predecessors, bestowed upon M. des Monts, in the year 1604, all this country from the 40th degree of latitude to the 46th. Since this grant the aforesaid Seigneur des Monts, in his own person and through

M. de Poutrincourt and thro' others, has often taken real possession of the whole country and this three years even before the English had set forth, or any one heard anything of this claim of theirs.' These and several other things the aforesaid Sieur. de Biancourt found out and made known, thus encouraging his people. I, for my part, had two other motives which urged me to this same voyage; one, to accompany, as spiritual assistant the aforesaid Sieur. de Biancourt, and his people, the other, to find out and to see myself the disposition of these nations to accept the Holy Gospel. These, then, were the motives of our voyage.

"We arrived at Kinnibéqui, 80 leagues from Port Royal, on the 28th October, the day of St. Simon and St. Jude of the same year 1611. Immediately, our men went on shore, desirous to see the fort of the English; for we had heard on the way, that there was no one there. Now, as at first everything looks fine, they went to work praising and boasting of this enterprise of the English and to enumerate the advantages of the place; everybody praised in it what he valued most. But a few days later they changed their views; for there was seen a fair chance of raising a counter-fort, which would have imprisoned them and cut them off from the river and the sea; item, that even if they had been left there, they would nevertheless not have enjoyed the commodities of the river, since it had several mouths and finer estuaries, at some distance from there. . . .

"But, since I have made mention of the English, some one may perchance wish to hear of their adventures, which we were told here. It is therefore, thus, that in the year 1608 the English, began to settle down at one of the mouths of this river Kennebec; as has been said before. They had then as their head a very honest man, who got along remarkable well with the natives of the country. They say, however, that the Armouche-quois were afraid of such neighbors, and on that account murdered this Captain, of whom I have spoken. These people are accustomed to this business, to kill people by Magic. Now in the second year, 1609, the English, under another Captain changed their policy. They repelled the natives and committed excesses of every kind, without much restraint; hence, these poor, ill-treated people impatient with the present, and fearing more from the future, resolved, so the saying is, to kill the whelp before he should have powerful claws and teeth. The opportunity offered one day, when their sloops had gone to a distant place, in order to fish. My conspirators followed them upon their track, and drawing near with many signs of friendship (for thus they always are most friendly when they are nearest to treachery) they entered and at a given signal, each man chose his man and killed him with his big knife. Thus perished eleven Englishmen. The others, intimidated abandoned their enterprise that same year, and have not continued it since, being content to come in the summer to fish near this island of Emetenic, which as we mentioned before was 8 leagues from the fort they had begun.

"On this account, therefore, the outrage committed in the person of Captain Platrier by said Englishmen, having been perpetrated on this island of Emetenic, M. de Biancourt considered the expediancy of going to reconnoitre it and to leave there some token of having reclaimed it. This he did by erecting in the harbour a very

FRENCH PLANTING A CROSS IN THE NEW WORLD
From an old drawing

fine cross, with the arms of France. Some of his people suggested to him to burn the sloops which he found there, but as he was gentle and humane, he would not do it, considering that they were not men-of-war but fishing vessels.

"From there since the season pressed us, for it was already November 6th we made sail to return to Port Royal, stopping at Pentegoet as we had promised the Savages.

"From Port Royal, the last of January, 1612, Pierre Biard."[52]

Here we have another cross, erected in Monhegan's harbor by the French, unless they, as is quite possible, simply substituted the colors of France for the English colors on the cross that was already standing. If this latter was the case, Biard would not have mentioned the English cross as standing, as they would not have desired the people at home to know that the English cross was already on this island, as the cross was always an evidence of ownership at that time. He speaks as if this cross was erected on Smutty Nose.

Capt. Edward Harlow, during the summer of 1611, while cruising in this neighborhood, called at Monhegan, and either from here or in the vicinity, seized three natives who had come on board for the purpose of trading; two of these he carried away, the other escaping. At Nono No, the Indian name for an island near Cape Cod, he captured another, continuing down the coast he kidnapped

[52] Brown, *Genesis of the United States*, vol. II, pp. 533-536. Biard evidently made a mistake in the years, 1608-9. He should have said 1607-8.

two more at Capawick, taking five in all to England.[53]

The Indians he took from Monhegan were named Pechmo, Monopet, and Pekenimine; Pechmo escaped. Epanow and Coneconum were the names of those taken from Capawick (Martha's Vineyard).

The Dutch were now extremely interested in this new world and were also sending out expeditions for discovery. Henry Hudson, in the employ of the Dutch East India Company, ranged the coast in July of 1609. Undoubtedly his *Half Moon* dropped her anchor in our harbor. At this time most voyagers stopped at any place where ships were known to be anchored for news and a chat with any shipmaster that might be there.

Hudson, from his acquaintanceship with the gossip and knowledge of English discovery of the time, could not have failed to have known of Monhegan.

The inns of the seaports of England were resorts of sailors, commanders and merchants, who employed ships in commerce, and as there were no other means of obtaining news in those days than by gossip and tales, we can be sure that every Englishman ranging the North American waters was well acquainted with this fishing island of Monhegan. Hudson was an Englishman. He is credited with having Waymouth's data and to have been advised by Capt. John Smith, then in the employ of the South Virginia Company. It is recorded that he made a

[53] From "Something about Monhegan," by E. H. Goss, in *Mag. of Am. Hist.*, vol. 12, p. 266, Jul.-Dec., 1884.

new foremast from one of the pine trees that lined the shore, and also that his crew became unruly and drove some of the natives from their homes with firearms and plundered them.

It is unfortunate for the historian that Gorges was such a modest man. He took so little credit to himself for his great efforts, painstaking letter writing and business management of the Second Colony of Virginia, that he has never been given the credit that is justly his due in the founding of New England. Posterity would not even have had the two brief accounts of these activities that he has left had not the First Colony of Virginia and his enemies forced him to defend the efforts made by him, and his associates, before Parliament and the King. We do not even have a record of a portrait, or likeness of any kind, having been made of him, an unusual occurrence for that time. He rather pathetically says: "I have spent 20,000 pounds of my estate, and thirty years the whole flower of my life, in new discoveries and settlements upon a remote continent."

That Gorges fully expected to come some day to this new country which he knew so intimately from reports, and that he also pleaded to be permitted to come, are matters of record and the attitude of many historians, even some of Maine's own, has been unbelievably biased as to his great contribution to the colonization of Maine.

The English were by this time fully aware of the intentions of the French to dispute the territory and were also determined to drive them out of their settlements in Canada and Nova Scotia, which the English claimed belonged to Virginia. For this purpose, Sir Samuel Argall was sent from the South Virginia Colony, with a commission and sufficient force to effectively accomplish the purpose. He destroyed the forts that they had built at Mount Mansell (Mount Desert), Saint Croix and Port Royal, took their guns and ammunitions, seized their ship, cattle and provisions and carried them away to Virginia, "where they were much needed." His exploit effectively expelled the French from the territory for the time.

We have a letter,[54] written by Father Pierre Biard, which tells of his experience and desire to reach Monhegan, in part:

"There was no time to lose. In this perplexity, each one did what he could for his safety. Father Ennemond Masse got with 14 others into the boat, (that Argall had allowed them to retain), of which we have spoken, and God protected him, as your Fatherhood has already heard.

"I went to see the English Commander; and obtained for myself and Father Jacques Quentin, my companion, as well as for Jean Dixon, who had been admitted unto the Society (Jesuits), and for one servant, that we should be carried to some island near by, where the English are

[54] Letter by Father Pierre Biard to the very Reverend Father Claude Acquaviva, General Society of Jesus, from Carayon's *Premiere Mission*, pp. 106-116, which is published in Brown's *Genesis of the United States*, vol. 2, p. 702.

in the habit of fishing, and that we should be recommended to these fishermen in order that they might carry us to England, from whence we could easily return to France. I obtained this, I say, as a promise, but they did not keep their word. In fact, we and the other Frenchmen who remained, fifteen in number, were taken straight to Virginia, nearly 250 post-leagues from where we were taken prisoners."

The English destroyed everywhere the monuments and all other evidences of the French Supremacy, according to Biard, and at Port Royal they went so far as to use a pick and chisel on a large massive stone on which were engraved the names of Sieur de Monts, with other captains, and also the lilies of France.

A charter covering the territory of Newfoundland had been granted by King James in 1610 to prominent merchants and adventurers, among whom was Abram Jennings and Thos. Aldworth, men who later were connected with Monhegan.

Gorges says in his *Briefe Relation*[55] that he had heard that "Sir William Alexander, Knight, and one of his Majesty's most honorable Councell of the Kingdome of Scotland," was granted Nova Scotia. He also says that this grant took away some of their "priuities," which evidently means some of their territory.

From 1608 until 1626, when there were several estab-

[55] *Gorges and His Province of Maine.* Prince ed., vol. 1, p. 208.

lished settlements in New England, voyages were so frequent to Monhegan, which seems to have been the port for most of the Second Colony for fishing and barter, and also as a port of call, that no attempt will be made to record all of them, but only such as have a bearing on our history.

The Vatican seems to have been interested in the English settlements here, for we find that gossip sent from Antwerp to the Vatican and found in the archives there tells of "12,000 English and Scots in Virginia in 1611," and also "that the English increase daily." Monhegan was still a part of North Virginia. Attempts at colonization were now in full swing. Fifty-four Englishmen, six women and two children are recorded as wintering in Newfoundland in 1613. Monhegan, too, was a substantial trading center, and other settlements were beginning on the mainland opposite.

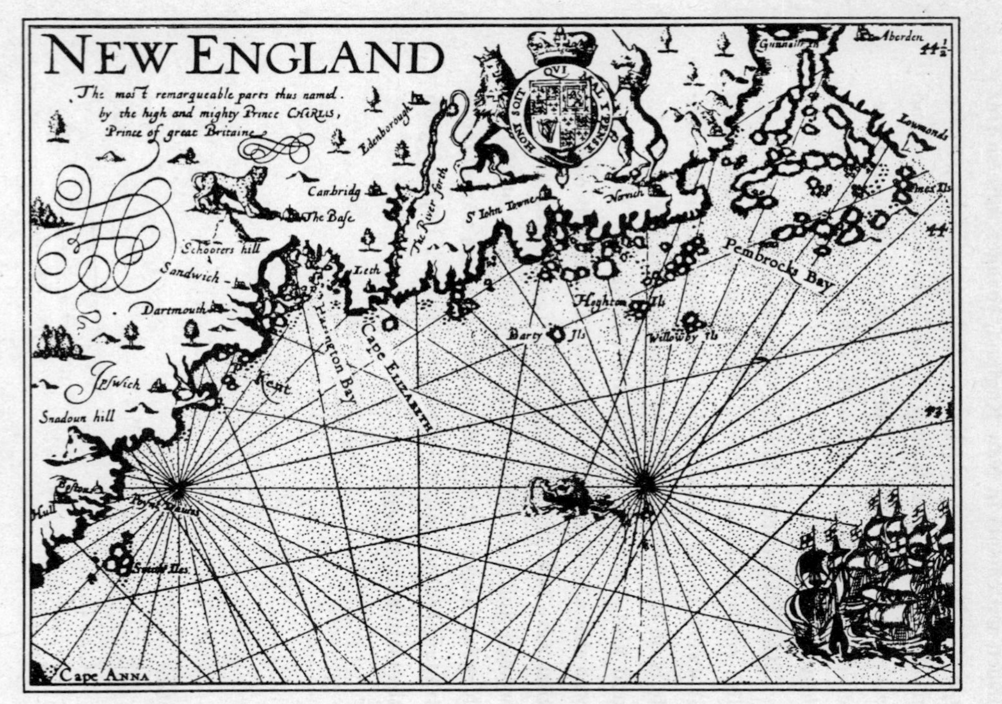

PORTION OF JOHN SMITH'S MAP OF NEW ENGLAND, FIRST STATE, 1614,
SHOWING MONHEGAN AS BARTY ILS

CHAPTER XI

A VERY distinguished visitor came to Monhegan in 1614. Today he would be called the "Publicity Agent of New England," Capt. John Smith. Being a ready writer and a keen observer he is competent to tell us about the island as he saw it in his own words:

"In the moneth of Aprill, 1614, with two Ships from *London* of a few Marchants, I chanced to arriue in *New-England*, a parte of *Ameryca*, at the Ile of *Monahigan* in 43½ of Northerly latitude; our plot was there to take Whales and make tryalls of a Myne of Gold and Copper. If those failed, Fish and Furres was then our refuge, to make our selues sauers howsoeuer; we found this Whale-fishing a costly conclusion: we saw many, and spent much time in chasing them, but could not kill any: They being a kinde of Iubartes, and not the Whale that yeeldes Finnes and Oyle as we expected. For our Golde, it was rather the Masters deuice to get a voyage that proiected it, than any knowledge he had at all of any such matter. Fish and Furres war now our guard: and by our late arriual and long lingering about the Whale(s), the prime of both these seasons, were past ere wee preceiued it; we thinking that their seasons serued at all times; but we found it otherwise; for, by the midst of Iune, the fishing failed. Yet in Iuly and August some were taken, but not sufficient to defray so great a charge as our stay required. Of dry fish we made about 4000. of Cor fish about 7000. whilst our sailors fished, myselfe with eight or nine others of them that might best be spared, Ranging the coast in a small boat, wee got for trifles neer 1100 Beaver skinnes, 100 Martine and neer as many Otters: and most of them within the distance of twenty leagues.

"We ranged the Coast both East and West much furder; but Eastwards our Commodities were not esteemed, they were so neare the French who affords them better: and right against vs in the Main was a Ship of Sir *Frances Popphames*, that had there such acquaintance, hauing many yeares used onely that porte, that the most part was had by him. And 40 leagues westward were two French Ships that had made there a great voyage by trade, during the time wee tryed those conclusions not knowing the Coast, nor Saluages habitations.

"With these Furres, the Traine and Cor-fish I returned to *England* in the Bark: where within six months after our departure from the *Downes*, we safe arriued back. The best of the fish was solde for five pounds the hundreth, the rest by ill vsage betwixt three pounds and fifty shillings.

"The other Ship staied to fit herselfe for *Spaine* with the dry fish which was soulde by the Sailors reporte that returned, at forty ryalls the quintall, each hundred weighing two quintalls and a halfe."[56]

[56] Smith, *Description of New England.* Arber ed., vol. 1, p. 187.

This other ship was commanded by Hunt, who after Smith left, seized upon twenty-seven natives, near Cape Cod, put them in the hold of the vessel and carried them away to Spain where he tried to sell them for slaves. This was probably the most unfortunate incident in the whole history of these times as we learn from Gov. Bradford's History, written several years later, who on Samoset's authority gives this account:

"This people are ill affected to us because of Hunt, who carried away twenty from this place we now inhabit, and seven from the Nausits."

Hunt carried these savages to Spain, but we learn from Gorges' account that the Spanish would not buy them for slaves when they found they were from America. But the outrage made more difficult the progress of colonization.

The Plymouth Company and the French had both treated the natives as friends and had done everything that they could to inspire in them a belief in their peaceful intentions. Especially was this true in the case of Gorges, who, not only had been very friendly to them, so that every one in England sent him any wandering Indians there, but he had studied them with care and his indignation at this outrage by Hunt is extreme, as can be learned from his story.[57]

To continue with John Smith's story, in which he makes some interesting observations in regard to the charts and "Relations" of others:

[57] *Briefe Relation. Gorges and His Province of Maine.* Prince ed., vol. 1, p. 209.

THE PORTRAICTUER OF CAPTAYNE IOHN SMITH ADMIRALL OF NEW ENGLAND.

MONHEGAN

"Northward six or seauen degrees is the River *Sagadahock,* where was planted the Westerne Colony, by that Honourable Patrone of vertue Sir *Iohn Poppham* Lord Chief Iustice of *England.* There is also a relation printed by Captaine *Bartholomew Gosnould,* of *Elizabeth's Isles*: and an other by Captaine *Waymouth* of *Pemmaquid.* From all these deligent obseruers, posterity may be bettered by the fruits of their labours. But for diuers others that long before and since haue ranged those parts, within a kenning sometimes of the shore, some touching in one place some another, I must entreat them pardon me for omitting them; or if I offend in saying that their true descriptions are concealed, or neuer well obserued, or died with the Authors: so that the Coast is yet (1616) still but euen as a Coast vnknowne and vndiscouered. I haue had six or seaven seuerall plots of those Northern parts, so vnlike each to other, and most so differing, from any true proportion, or resemblance of the Countrey, as they did mee no more good, then so much waste paper, though they cost me more. It may be it was not my chance to see the best; but least others may be deceiued as I was, or through dangerous ignorance hazard themselues as I did, I haue drawen a Map from Point to Point, Ile to Ile, and Harbour to Harbour, with the Soundings, Sands, Rocks, and Land-marks as I passed close aboard the Shore in a little Boat; although there be many things to bee obserued which the haste of other affaires did cause mee to omit: for, being sent more to get present commodities, then knowledge by discoueries for any future good, I had not power to search as I would: Yet it will serve to direct any shall goe that waies, to safe Harbours and the Saluages habitations: what marchandize and commodities for their labour they may finde, this following discourse shall plainely demonstrate. . . .

"The remarkeablest Iles and Mountains for Landmarkes are these: the highest Ile is *Sorico* in the Bay of *Pennobscot*, but the three Iles, and a rock of *Matinnack* are much furder in the Sea: *Metinicus* is also three plaine Iles and a rock, betwixt it and *Monahigan*. *Monahigan* is a round high Ile, and close by it *Monanis*, betwixt which is a small harbor where wee ride."[58] . . .

". . . high, craggy Cliffy, Rocks, stony Isles, that I wondered such great trees could growe vpon so hard foundations. . . ." "yet the Sea there is the strangest fishpond I euer saw. The coast mountainous, and isles of huge rocks, overgrown with most sorts of excellent good woods for house building."

He describes the fertility of Monhegan's soil which we residents of the Island all know well enough:

"Yet I made a Garden vpon the top of a Rockie Ile in 43½, 4 leagues from the Main, in May, that grew so well, as it served vs with sallets in Iune and Iuly."

As for the fishing he tells of the advantages of the Island:

"In March, Aprill, May and halfe Iune, here is Cod in

[58] Smith, *Description of New England.* Arber ed., vol. 1, p. 198.

abundance; in May, Iune, Iuly and August, Mullet and Sturgion, whose roes doe make Cauiare and Puttargo. Herring, if any desire them, I haue taken many out of the bellies of Cods, some in nets, but the Saluages compare their store in the Sea, to the haires of their heads: and surely there are an incredible abundance vpon this Coast. In the end of August, September, October and Nouember you haue Cod againe, to make Cor fish, or Poore Iohn; and each hundred (fish) is as good as two or three hundred in *Newfoundland*: so that halfe the labour in hooking, splitting, and turning is saued. And you may haue your fish at what market you will, before they can haue any in *New-found-Land*; where their fishing is chiefly in Iune and Iuly: whereas it is heere in March, Aprill, May, September, October and November, as is said. So that by reason of this plantation, the Marchants may haue fraught (freight) both out and home: which yeelds an aduantage worth consideration."

Here he speaks as if there was an established station at Monhegan, in 1614, as we have already noted as having been established in 1608 or 1609.

In *New England Trials* Smith recounts the success of twenty-six ships employed thither, "within these six years with the benefit of that country by sea and land and how to build three score Sayle of good ships to make a little Navie Royale."

He must have obtained these figures from Gorges or some of his associates. And this seems reasonable for after his return to England he got in touch with the men of the Second Colony and they commissioned him a Rear Admirall for New England, for life. His story continues:

"With two shippes I went from the Downes, the third of March (1614) *and arriued in* New England *the last of Aprill. I had but fortie fiue men and boyes: We built seuen boates. 37 did fish; my selfe with eight others ranging the coasts, I tooke a plot of what I could see, got acquaintance of the inhabitants, . . ."*[59]

Smith locates the dwelling of the Bashabes and says of the Indians:

"All of these I could perceiue, differ little in language, fashon, or gouerment: though most be Lords of themselues, yet they hold the Bashabes of Penobscot the chiefe and greatest amongst them."

During 1614, while Smith was ranging our coasts, another expedition was being set on foot by Gorges, for he says that while he was considering the best means of reviving his languishing hopes of colonization, Capt. Henry Harley brought to him one of the Indians who, as we now know, had been captured by Harlow in 1611. This savage, named Epenow, had been exhibited in London for a wonder, "being a goodly man of brave aspect." Epenow was well acquainted with the Indian tribes of New England.

At about the same time Gorges had recovered "his Indian," Assacumet, one of the Waymouth captives, whom Gorges had sent with "Challounge" on his unfortunate

[59] Smith, *New England Trials.* Ed. 1, proof 1.

expedition, who had been carried to Spain in 1606. He lodged the two Indians together and, in his *Brief Narration*, he says that they did not understand each other, but that their difference in speech "was no more then that as ours is betweene the Northern and Southerne people."

With these Indians Sir Ferdinando hoped to accomplish something, so with the Earl of Southampton, who was at this time very powerful in England, they fitted out a ship which was put in command of a "grave gentleman," recommended by the Earl, "one Captaine Hobson, who was willing to go that voyage and to adventure 100 £ himselfe."

Another Indian, Wanape, or possibly Manawet, who had been sent to Gorges from the Isle of Wight, was also secured for the voyage.

Monhegan was undoubtedly the landfall of this voyage which set out in June, 1614. Epenow, with the cunning of his race, had described a mine of gold and had promised to locate it for them. He was undoubtedly actuated by his knowledge of the desires of the English for this metal, and told the tale in order to get back to his own people, although we find later that there was such a mine.

It may have been while they were in the Monhegan harbor that Epenow learned of the capture by Hunt of twenty of his tribe for he was on hearing of it filled with hatred of the whole English race, as Gorges relates. At any rate Epenow escaped later and the voyage was not successful.

On Smith's return to England he must, as we have already said, established communications with Sir Ferdinando Gorges, as in his *Description of New England* he says:

"At last it pleased Sir *Ferdinando Gorge* and Master Doctor *Sut(c)liffe,* Deane of Exceter, to conceiue so well of these proiects and my former imployments, as induced them to make a new aduenture with me in those parts, whither they haue so often sent to their continuall losse."

Smith's enthusiasm for the country belonging to the North Virginia Council aroused not only that company to new efforts, but the Londoners offered Smith the command of their ships, which he declined, having already made a life-engagement. Nevertheless three London ships sailed in January, led by Capt. Michel Cooper, and reached Monhegan in March, 1615, where they fished until June and then sent a ship to Spain loaded with fish. This ship was taken by the Turks, while another ship sailed for Virginia, leaving the third to return to England with fish and oil.[60]

The Plymouth or Second Colony of Virginia, who had as president that year, 1615, Sir Richard Hawkins, a former mayor of Bristol, sent out another expedition, headed by him. He sailed in October and arrived at Monhegan when the Indian War was at its height and during which the Bashaba, who was so friendly to the English, was

[60] DeCosta, *Norumbega and its English Explorers.* Winsor's *Narrative and Critical History of the United States.*

killed, along with many of the sagamores. Hawkins got what he could in barter and fish and sailed to Spain, "to make the most of such commodities as he had got together," which Sir Ferdinando says, "was all that was done by any of us that year."

Smith tells us, nevertheless, that Plymouth in 1616 sent out four ships and London two; while Purchas states that "eight voluntaire shipe" went to New England to make "further tryall." Another of 200 tons, the *Nachen*, commanded by Edwarde Brawnde, who wrote to "his worthye good frend Captayne John Smith, admiral of New England," also went out. In his letter to Smith he refers to other vessels on the coast. The *Nachen*, of London, sailed from Dartmouth March 8 and reached Monhegan April 20. Afterward Captain Brawnde went to Cape Cod in his pinnace in search of pearls. Brawnde also says that he had his boats appropriated by Sir Richard Hawkins, who wintered at Monhegan and sailed to Virginia in the spring.

In spite of mishaps Brawnde thought well of New England where profitable voyages were to be made in fish and furs, "if not spoiled by two many factors." Factors were men sent over to trade with the Indians. He found the climate good enough and the savages "a gentell-natured people," a result obtained by Gorges' unfailing kindness to them.

In 1615 Smith was appointed Admiral of New England for life, and he succeeded in securing two ships, with Master Dermer and others with him, and as Gorges says:

". . . to lay the foundation of a new Plantation, and to try the fishing of that Coast, and to seeke to settle a trade with the Natiues: But such was his misfortune, as being scarse free of our owne Coast, he had his masts shaken ouerboard by stormes and tempests, his ship wonderfully distressed, and in that extremity forced to come back againe; so as the season of the yeere being almost spent, we were of necessitie enforced to furnish him with another ship, and taking out the prouissons of the first, dispatched him away againe, who comming to the height of the Westerne Islands, was chased by a French Pirate, and by him made prisoner, although his ship in the night escaped away, and returned home with the losse of much of her prouision, and the ouer-throw of that voyage, to the ruine of that poore Gentleman Captaine Smith who was detained prisoner by them, and forced to suffer many extremities, before hee got free of his troubles."

Smith was chased by English and French pirates but was finally captured by French men-of-war.

From 1609 to 1616 Vines and some of Gorges' servants and perhaps some of his numerous relatives seem to have been quartered on the island. As near as can be found out, during these years, salt works were established near Green Point, for want of salt is never mentioned by anyone afterwards, and a house for the tenders was built just above it. The remains of the chimney of this house is still there, but trees of large growth are growing in the midst of the bricks of the chimney. It was near the site of a house occupied at a much later period by one Brooks.

In 1616-1617 the pestilence ranged the coast, which cleared the country of Indians to such an extent that the settlers seem to have grown bolder and to have reached out in every direction soon after Dermer's voyage.

Sir Walter Raleigh, who had made such heroic efforts to colonize America and who had been languishing in the London Tower, was released and sailed away for a trip to this country, which formerly had belonged to him. During 1617-18, therefore, while John Smith was still boosting the Northern Colony in England, Raleigh sailed along the whole coast of the United States and probably visited all the harbors between Virginia and Newfoundland. He arrived in England in June of 1618 and was immediately arrested and executed. But he lived to see the country being settled, as he had prophesied that he would. Undoubtedly he stopped at his cousin's, Gorges', trading post on Monhegan.

By this time Monhegan must have had quite a number of log houses scattered in convenient places, close by the little beaches, but sheltered from the too curious observations of passing crafts, behind Manana. The sloping ground toward the meadow must have been filled with flake racks; huge trees covered the hillsides to the east and the heads, while Manana must have thrown her shadows well over the island in the late afternoon. Wintering on Monhegan had now become the usual practice, and gardens were undoubtedly planted and tended.

The Second Colony had by this time established a regular schedule for her fishing ships and trade. Boats came laden with provisions and articles for trade, or truck, with the Indians, such sailors or craftsmen as were needed, and other necessities, and returned with the fish and furs. That there were numerous Indians quartered on the Island is recorded by Gorges in his *Briefe Relation,* among whom was undoubtedly Samoset.

While most of the Adventurers of this Second Colony were evidently interested in the trade in fish and furs, Gorges appears to have been always thinking of colonization. In consequence he records the voyages for exploration much more fully than he does the activities of the fishing station. These fishing operations we find only upon close study of his two narratives. He will speak of the vessels going to the "usual place" for fishing, when he speaks of the place of rendezvous.

The "usual place" is Monhegan, but whether he had become so habituated to concealing this place, or was not satisfied with the designation of Waymouth, "Ile St. George," or the name of Monhegan confused him as apparently did all Indian names, it is hard to learn at this remote period. It is only after John Smith's return that he uses the name Menehighon for the Island. Probably secrecy was no longer necessary after John Smith's publications were broadcast.

The maps of the early sixteenth century, although vague, as Capt. John Smith has so justly said, yet have often suggestive marks and names, that in view of Monhegan's later history show that the older explorers were well acquainted with her.

The Portuguese map of Cantino, 1500, or Corte Reals' map, shows a little island off "Cabo-d-lictute" and the Baye of St. Jhan Baptiste that may have been intended for Monhegan. A map made from Fagundes' voyage shows an island in this vicinity; Agnese, in his Portulanus Atlas, shows a vague outline of the Gulf of Maine with small islands strongly marked. On the Italian map of Gastaldi, 1550, Louise might have been Monhegan; on Ortelius' "World Map, 1570, Nordenskiod Facsimile Atlas," Claudia is placed in this location. We know that Ortelius knew considerable about Norumbega and as this place has been quite definitely located as the Penobscot, he may have intended Claudia for Monhegan. Mercator follows Ortelius in locating Claudia. Almost all of the old maps, that have the "wind roses," either a rose will be placed in Monhegan's position or will have a direct wind line running to the locality.

Monhegan is spelled in innumerable ways in the old records: Manhegin, Monahan, Menehighon, Monhigen, Monhagen, Monhiggen, Monhiggon, Munhiggon, Monahiggan, Monnahigen, Menhiggen, Menhiggon, Munhiggon, Manaheigan, Mapahiggon, Quamphegon, Munhigon, Monheghen, and various other ways.

Other names she bore were: Brisa (meaning windy, which would be very appropriate), St. George, La Nef,

Ile of Shipps, Ile of Schiffe, E. Mmentinic, Batties, Barty's, Ile of Bacchus, King James his Iles (Dermer's name), Southack's Island (Drake), and numerous others.

The derivation of the name Monhegan has never been seriously studied by any philologist of note, so far as this search has extended. The people who consulted the Indians for its meaning received the information, as might have been expected, that it meant an island in the sea. Of course it meant that to them. But had it really been derived from some Indian word we would have had other instances of its use applied to other islands in the sea.

In one authority is found the definition of the words "a little stone," in the Indian language of the region, "Mananst." In this same authority "a sword" is called "Monhacan." These two words might easily have been the origin of the names of our islands. The sword found by the Corte Reals' vessel might have been picked up at Monhegan.

C. E. Potter, in an appendix to *Language of Abnaquies,* says: "Monhegan and Monanas are undoubtedly corruptions for Monahan or Monan. Grand and Petit Monahans, being the Indian nouns with French adjectives.

Often in the old records the name of the Island is spelled Mohegan, and also the Mohegan Indians are often recorded as the Monhegan Indians. Of course *mañana* is the Spanish word for tomorrow.

There is a strange relationship between Monhegan and Ireland. A great many of the English people interested in the discovery and colonization of this part of North

America were also interested in the colonization of Ireland; in fact, the colonization of Ireland set the pace for the colonization of North America. It is possible that the name Monhegan was given the island by Sir Humphrey Gilbert. He had been in service in Ireland from 1566 to 1570, during which time he was made Governor of Munster. In 1566 he was told of the Northwest Passage by "Salva terra." Sir John Popham was interested in Irish colonization, which was considered as hazardous as that of America.

Sir Hugh Wirrall, one of the Adventurers of the Second Colony, settled a plantation in Ireland called "Monaghan," which pronounced in the flat English of the time would sound not unlike Monhegan to the Indians. The word "Monaghan" has been explained as meaning in Irish hills or surrounded by hills. It may easily have been given to the Island by some of the early Irish voyagers, of legendary fame, when they landed in the region, or by early English voyagers.

There is also the name given to at least a part of Maine, or the Bashaba's country, by Gorges called "Moasham," by Smith, "Moshoquen," by Samuel Purchas, "Mawooshen," and by Samoset later, "Moratiggon." Biard gives the definition of the country:

"Virginia is that continent which the ancients called *Morosa*, between Florida and New France under the 36°, 37°, and 38° degrees of N. L."[61]

[61] Biard's *Relation*. Brown's *Genesis of the United States*, vol. 2.

Samoset, as will appear during the course of this story, always mixed his foreign words. This name appears to have had a Celtic origin. Humboldt said that, "Traces of Celtic have been discovered by some of the philologists, when put to the task, in the American language."

John Smith seems to have published his *Description of New England* in 1616, and *New England Trials* in 1620. In the latter he shows his greater enthusiasm for this part of the English possessions in the new world than for the Virginia Colony. He states: That he would rather live here in New England "than any of the four parts of the world," that he has "yet seen not inhabited."

His map, of which he is justly proud, being shown to Prince Charles, later King Charles I, His Majesty promptly renamed most of the islands, bays, rivers, capes and the country generally. But the name of New England given by Smith was retained. King Charles bestowed most of the names but Smith seems to have given the name Barty Iles to Monhegan. Other maps of the time give the spelling as Battes Island. "Peckham (Sir George) in a marginal note to his Westerne Planting, enumerates the English voyagers to America, and among them mentions William Battes. He was probably the man who was selected by Humpfy Gilbert to make the preliminary voyage."[62]

This adventurer may have been the man Capt. John Smith wished to honor, and the connection of his name

[62] *Merchant Adventurers with Sir Humphrey Gilbert.*

with Monhegan lends strength to the faint indications that one, at least, of Sir Humphrey's adventurers landed on Monhegan. The spelling of proper names was not a fine art among the early cartographers and narrators.

If all these old-world legends of voyages that have been enumerated were true, it would at last settle the question of why the native tribes were at such enmity, one with the other, when the European voyagers came to the shores of North America. All the early voyagers record these deadly feuds, and give the same locations to the various tribes. It is well within the bounds of possibility that the Norsemen, deadly enemies of the Irish, as has been related, may have settled and mingled with the natives of "Norumbega," while the Irish may well have been the "Papas" living in the region of the Kennebec, and westward, while the Welsh may have intermingled with the natives lower down the coast, or vice versa.

The reasons for these reflections arise out of the careful reading of early records and also from the fact, now so well known, that in other parts of the American continent it was the common thing for the European man to go native, to take an Indian wife, and in consequence the histories and tales are filled with the term "squaw man," applied to such a person, and half-breeds were extremely common. As late as 1890 the term was commonly applied, to such men, on the Pacific Coast who lived with the Siwash squaws. John Smith tells of the French "that liue with those people as one nation or family." Human nature was certainly not very different three or four hundred years before. We have also the tales of Ari, son of Mar, who went to "Irland it Mikland" and how he became a chief there. Castine married an Indian wife, Rolfe of Virginia married Pocahontas, and certain old Virginia families pride themselves on having her for an ancestor. It would be remarkable had not those early voyagers mingled with the natives in such a remote place, and have instilled their hatreds into the tribes along with their blood. There are also many instances of the Indians adopting the language used by the fishermen of different nationalities. The European fishermen had a jargon, a seaman's slang, which included apt words from the various languages spoken by the fishermen of the other countries, just as obtains today among soldiers and sailors stationed in such surroundings as were these men.

This theory would also account for the decided characteristics of the Indians. Some of them were more interested in fish and furs, others in agricultural pursuits, or arts, traits that they may have received from their European ancestry.

To get back to the voyagers: Dermer seems to have arrived safely at Monhegan, to have loaded the ship with the fish and furs and sailed with her as far as Newfoundland on her homeward way. While at Monhegan information came to him about that mine of gold at an island called "Capawacke," off the Massachusetts shore, which tale Smith had discounted.

At Newfoundland, where Dermer spent nearly a year, he found Tisquantum, one of Hunt's captives, who had been brought by a Bristol vessel from Spain, and who evidently confirmed the statements of the treacherous Epenow regarding the mine at "Capawacke." Dermer sent this information to Gorges and suggested an arrangement which included his going back to Monhegan to meet a company with a commission, which he hoped Gorges would send over, for the purpose of making a reconnaissance of the island where the mine was located.

At this time Captain Mason was governor of Newfoundland, and advised Dermer to return to England to talk matters over with Gorges and his associates. So Dermer, unable to get back to Monhegan, took Mason's advice and went to England. In the meantime Gorges had sent Rocraft, a friend and former companion of Smith's, with a company for exploration, in the fishing ship and so Dermer missed Rocraft when the latter reached Monhegan.

Rocraft, not finding Dermer at Monhegan as he had expected, but finding a French "Barke of Deepe," "a fishing in a creek," seized her with the crew and master. Rocraft kept the "Barke," returning the French crew to England with the regular return voyage of the fishing vessel, on which he had come.

When these Frenchmen arrived in England, Gorges indemnified the Frenchman for his damage suffered, as his excuse that "he was of our religion."

With this bark and his company, Rocraft decided to stay for the winter on the coast, as he had salt and other necessities sufficient for the season. While he was cruising along some of his crew hatched a conspiracy to kill him, and to capture the ship and provisions, which plot Rocraft finding out about, caught them at the moment they had planned to execute their design. Hesitating to kill them, he landed them at Casco, with arms, ammunition, and some food, hoping that they might still be of some use in exploring or in making some discovery.

The men made their way back to Monhegan where they spent the winter with "bad lodging and worse fare," as Gorges says, but they finally arrived safely in England excepting one sickly man who died on the island. This is the first recorded death on Monhegan.

Rocraft's voyage to Virginia and the mishaps he encountered there, where he died and his bark was lost, are interesting as showing the hazards of the time, but do not further deal with the history of Monhegan.

In the meantime Gorges had sent Dermer, who had been bitten by the gold bug, back to Monhegan. On his way he picked up Tisquantum at Newfoundland, and from a letter which Dermer wrote to Purchas, we have an account of his search for the gold mine. It is a long letter, so only the portion pertaining to Monhegan will be quoted:

"To his Worshipfull Friend, M. Samuel Purchas, Preacher of the Word at the Church a little within Ludgate, London.

"Sir,—It was the nineteenth of May, before I was fitted for my discouery, when from Monahiggan I set sayle in an open Pinnace of five tun, for the Iland I told you of. I passed alongst the Coast where I found some ancient Plantations (Indian), not long since populous now vtterly void; in other places a remnant remaines, but not free of sicknesse. Their disease the Plague, for wee might perceiue the sores of some that had escaped, who described the spots of such as vsually die. When I arriued at my sauages natiue country (finding all dead) I travelled alongst adaies journey Westward, to a place called Nummastaquyt, where finding Inhabitants, I dispatched a Messenger a dayes journey further West to Poconackit which bordereth on the sea; whence came to see me two Kings, attended with a guard of fiftie armed men, who being well satisfied with that my Sauage and I discourfed vnto them (being desirous of noueltie) gaue mee content in whatsoeuer I demanded, where I found that former relations were true. Here I redeemed a Frenchman, and afterwards another at Mastachusit who three yeeres since escaped shipwracke at the North-east of Cape Cod, I must (amongst many things worthy of obseruation) for want of leisure, therefore hence I passe (not mentioning any place where we touched in the way) to the Iland, which we discouered the twelfth of June. Here we had good quarter with the Sauages, who likewise confirmed former reports. I found seuen seuerall places digged, sent home of the earth, with samples of other commodities elsewhere found, sounded the Coast, and the time being farre spent bare vp for Monnahiggan, arriuing the three and (twen)-tieth of June, where wee found our Ship ready to depart. To this Ile are two other neere adjoyning, all of which I called by the name of King James his Iles, because from thence I had the first motiues to search, For that which may hereafter be both honorable and profitable to his Majestie."

Dermer's reason for naming Monhegan "King James his Iles" was probably that he knew from Capt. John Smith that English names were to be given to the plantations, islands and country generally. He seems to have had considerable authority, as the "Admirall for life," Capt. John Smith, was tossing in the French warship, a prisoner, but busily engaged in writing his descriptions of New England.

Dermer sent the ships home, but as it was necessary to leave a sufficient number of men for defence, he shipped his provisions by the *Samson,* of Captain Ward, which was going to Virginia, and continued his discoveries along the coast in a small boat with a few men. On this trip he may have taken Samoset. He arrived in Virginia after having encountered a fight with the Indians, in which Epenow figured, was terribly wounded and fell ill of the sickness that Gorges says so many of the Englishmen contracted on the coast, and finally died before he regained Monhegan. Gorges felt so discouraged with this disaster that he thought that he would give the whole thing up. But he did not give up but began to plan for a new charter for the Second Colony that would be better fitted for the colonization scheme.

CHAPTER XII

WHILE Gorges and his associates were struggling with their plantation and fishing voyages, the South Virginia Company, residing in London near the seat of government, had reconstructed their charter twice, and as Gorges found after so many trials that if the peace, which Dermer had secured with the Indians of the coast, was to last, stronger measures for protecting and governing the new territories must be taken. All sorts of nondescript persons were "squatting" and fishing in the territory belonging to the Second Colony, unscrupulous merchants from every port were at Monhegan with disturbing consequence to the peaceful pursuits of the authorized fishing expeditions. As has been noted the outrages on the Indians were committed by masters and crews of ships sent out by others than the legitimate owners of the Second Charter.

Gorges, therefore, with the help of some influential titled persons, secured a new charter giving the new name of New England to the Colony. This "Council for New England," as it was popularly called, was incorporated on the 30th of November, 1620, under the name of "The Council Established at Plymouth, County of Devon, for the planting, ruling, ordering, and governing of New England in America."[63] The Council consisted of forty

[63] This patent can be found in Hazard's *Hist. Coll.*, vol. 1, pp. 103-118.

patentees, most of whom were persons of distinction: Thirteen of them were peers, some of the highest rank. The royal gift carried with it a valuable monopoly of the fisheries.

The Council decided to attract colonists through a history of the colony. This account, written by Gorges, *A briefe Relation of the Descovery and Plantation of New England,* was published by the Council in 1622.

The reservation of the fishing and flaking privileges were so bitterly opposed by the Virginia Colony that three times Gorges was hailed before Parliament and the King to explain and defend the new charter. It was a complicated and bitter fight, and while it affected the growing colony on Monhegan, it is a too well-known controversy to give in a history of the Island.

While the new charter was in course of birth, the Virginia Colony of London had granted permission for the unfortunate religious sect, who had been exiled in Holland, through their desire to worship God according to their beliefs, to settle near New York, the territory where the Dutch had settled without authority. These colonists, the Pilgrim Fathers, through good fortune, or the connivance of the master of the ship *Mayflower,* Jones, who we now know had been hired by the Dutch to keep them away from their trading post in New York, were landed in the region from which Hunt had taken twenty of his captives to Spain, and where the plague had entirely depopulated the land of the remains of the tribe. These Indians had been agriculturists and had cleared some fields, which the Pilgrims proceeded to plant, in the following spring.

We now come to Samoset and his welcome and connection with them. The name Samoset had quite evidently been given him by the people on Monhegan, after the name of Somersetshire or Somerset. It is spelled in various ways in the old records, but it has come down to us more oftenly spelled Samoset. This spelling we will adopt.

Dermer may have convoyed Samoset, Sagamore of Moratiggon, down the coast along with Tisquantum on the conciliatory voyage to the Indian tribes, located at the point where Hunt captured so many of them, and where they were so filled with hatred toward the English. However that may have been, he arrived at the point near where the Pilgrim Fathers landed, eight months before that historic event. The story of his good will, courage and civility toward the English is recorded in the words of Governor Bradford, and as he identifies himself with the English fishing station at Monhegan, we will quote his actions directly from the old records of the Pilgrims themselves as found in *Mourt's Relation*[64] as follows:

"Mar. 16, 1621. Friday the 16, a fair warm day towards. This morning we determined to conclude of the military orders, which we had begun to consider of before, but were interrupted by the savages as we mentioned formerly. And whilst we were busied hereabout,

[64] *Mourt's Relation.* By Bradford and Winslow. London, 1622.

we were interrupted again; for there presented himself a savage, which caused an alarm. He very boldly came all alone, and along the houses, straight to the rendez-vous; where we intercepted him, not suffering him to go in, as undoubtedly he would out of his boldness. He saluted us in English, and bade us Welcome!; for he had learned some broken English among the Englishmen that came to fish at Monhiggon, and knew by name most of the captains, commanders, and masters, that usually came. He was a man free in speech, so far as he could express his mind, and of seemly carriage. We questioned him of many things; he was the first savage we could meet withal. He said he was not of these parts, but of Morattiggon, and one of the sagamores or lords thereof; and had been eight months in these parts, it laying hence a day's sail with a great wind, and five days by land. He discourses of the whole country, and of every province and of their sagamores, and the number of men and strength. The wind beginning to rise a little, we cast a horseman's coat about him for he was stark naked, only a leather about his waist with a fringe about a span or little more. He had a bow and two arrows, the one headed, and the other unheaded. He was a tall straight man, the hair of his head black, long behind, only short before, none on his face at all. He asked some beer, but we gave him strong water and biscuit, and butter, and cheese, and pudding, and a piece of mallard; all which he liked well, and had been acquainted with such amongst the English. He told us where we now live is called Patuxet, and that about four years ago all the inhabitants died of an extraordinary plague, and there is neither man, woman, nor child remaining, as indeed we have found none; so there is none to hinder our possession, or to lay claim unto it. All the afternoon we spent in communication with him. We would gladly have been rid of him at night but he was not willing to go this night. Then we thought to carry him on shipboard wherewith he was well content, and went into the shallop; but the wind was high and the water scant that it could not return back. We lodged him that night at Steven Hopkin's house and watched him.

"The next day he went away back to the Masasoits from whence he said he came, who are our next bordering neighbours. They are sixty strong, as he saith. The Nausites are as near Southeast of them, and are a hundred strong, and those were they of whom our people were encountered as we before related. They are much incensed and provoked against the English; and about eight months ago slew three Englishmen, and two more hardly escaped by flight to Monhiggon. They were Sir Ferdinando Gorge's men, as this savage told us; as he did likewise of the huggery, that is, fight, that our discoverers had with the Nausites, and of our tools that were taken out of the woods, which we willed him should be brought again; otherwise we would right ourselves. These people are ill affected towards the English by reason of one Hunt, a master of a ship, who deceived the people and got them

SAMOSET AND THE PILGRIMS

From Brownell's *Indian Races of North and South America*

under color of trucking with them, twenty out of this place where we inhabit, and seven men from the Nausites, and carried them away, and sold them for slaves, like a wretched man (for twenty pounds a man,) that cares not what mischief he doth for his profit.

"Mar. 17. Saturday in the morning, we dismissed the savage and gave him a knife, a bracelet, and a ring. He promised within a night or two to come again and to bring with him some of the Massasoyts, with such beaver's skins as they had to truck with us.

"Saturday and Sunday reasonable fair days. On this day came again the savage, and brought with him five other tall, proper men. They had every man a deer's skin on him, and the principal of them had a wild cat's skin, or such like, on the one arm. They had most of them long hosen up to their groins, close made, and above their groins to the waist another leather; they were altogether like the Irish trowsers. [Another Irish touch.] They are of complexion like our own English gipseys; no hair or very little on their faces; on their heads long hair to their shoulders, only cut before; some trussed up before with a feather, broad-wise like a fan; another a fox tail hanging out. These left (according to our charge given him before) their bows and arrows a quarter of a mile from our town. We gave them entertainment as we thought was fitting them. They did eat liberally of our English victuals. They made semblance unto us of friendship and amity. They sang and danced after their manner, like antics. They brought with them in a thing like a bow case, (which the principal of them had about his waist,) a little of their corn pounded to powder, which, put in a little water they eat. He had a little tobacco in a bag; but none of them drank but when he liked. Some of them had their faces painted black, from the forehead to the chin, for or five fingers broad; others after other fashions, as they liked. They brought three or four skins; but we would not truck with them at all that day, but wished them to bring more, and we would truck for all; which they promised within a night or two, and would leave these behind them, though we were not willing they should; and they brought us all our tools again, which were taken in the woods, in our men's absence. So, because of the day we dismissed them as soon as we could. But Samoset, our first acquaintance either was sick or feigned himself so, and would not go with them, and stayed with us till Wednesday morning. Then we sent him to them, to know the reason they came not according to their words; and we gave him a hat, a pair of stockings and shoes, a shirt, and a piece of cloth to tie about his waist. The Sabbath day, when we sent them from us, we gave every one of them some trifles, especially the principal of them. We carried them, along with our arms to the place where they left their bows and arrows; where at they were amazed, and two of them began to slink away, but that the others called them. When they took their arrows we bade them farewell, and they were glad; and so, with many thanks given us, they departed with promise they would come again. Monday and Tuesday proved fair days, we digged our grounds and sowed our garden seeds.

"Wednesday a fine warm day. We sent away Samoset.

"Thursday, the 22 of March, was a fair warm day. About noon we met again about our public business. But we had scarce been an hour together but Samoset came again, and Squanto,[65] the only native of Patuxet, where we now inhabit, who was one of the twenty captives that by Hunt were carried away, and had been in England, and dwelt in Cornhill with Master John Slanie, a merchant, and could speak a little English, with three others; and they brought with them some few skins to truck, and some red herrings, newly taken and dried, but not salted and treaty.

"Samoset and Squanto, they stayed all night with us.

"Friday was a very fair day. Samoset and Squanto still remained with us. Squanto went at noon to fish for eels. At night he came home with as many as he could well lift in one hand; which our people were glad of, they were fat and sweet. He trod them out with his feet, and so caught them with his hands, without any other instrument."

Of the Indians in this region of Maine there seems to have been two main divisions or clans. The Etchemins and the Abenakis. The Abenakis, who are said by one authority never to have acknowledged any Indian ancestry,

[65] Squanto is the Tisquantum of the Dermer voyage.

were divided into four main tribes: The Sekokis, or Saco; the Anasagunticooks; the Canibas or Kennebec; the Wawenocks. When Gorges first settled his trading post on Monhegan the Bashaba was ruler over the Abenakis. Johnston says that the Bashaba probably belonged to the Wawenocks, the tribe having its fishing and hunting grounds between the Kennebec and the St. Croix Rivers. This agrees with the old authorities. The word Abenaki (Wanbanboghi or more literally Wan ban ban) meant, according to one authority, the people of the Aurora Borealis.

The Etchemins had three principal tribes: The Penobscots or Tarrantines; the Passamaquoddy; and the Malecites. These tribes were allied to the French interests, and were, even before the advent of the Europeans in the sixteenth century, deadly enemies of the Abenakis.

Samoset was probably of the Wawenock tribe, and a sagamore, or chief of one division of it. Does not the word sagamore sound like a form of the word saga of the Norse language? Sagas has a similar sound to your author's ear.

The Abenaki tribe was less warlike than the other tribes and certainly was decidedly friendly to the English adventurers. John Smith says of these Indians: ". . . they were very active, strong, healthful and very wittie. The men had a perfect constitution of body, were of comely proportions and quite athletic. They would row their canoes faster with five paddles than our men would row our boat with eight oars."

One old writer says: "The country is possessed by divers sorts of People judged to be Tartars by Descent which are divided into several tribes, the *Churchers,* Tarentines, and Monhegans to the last and north-east."

"It is said that Tappan's Island, near Damariscotta, was the burial place of the Monhegan Indians, whose skeletons are found about two feet beneath the surface; their uniform position is with the knees drawn up, and the face to the East. Sometimes sheets of copper were placed over their heads — one of them had a copper knife blade set in a bone handle."[66]

But troubles with charters and difficulties of the Council do not seem to have disturbed the plantation at Monhegan, even if it did disturb Gorges. Ships came and went on regular schedule each year, and some spent the winter at the Island.

The Plymouth Plantation had been augmented by thirty-seven persons who came without provisions in the *Fortune.* When, therefore, a shallop belonging to the ship *Sparrow,* sent by Thomas Weston, came into their harbor with six or seven more improvident colonists, Edward Winslow was dispatched to "Munhiggen" to obtain supplies from the fishing fraternity whose rendezvous was evidently there. He says that "there were above thirty Sail of ships that fished, at Damarin's Cove, near Mun-

[66] Dr. Charles T. Jackson's 3rd Annual Report on Geology of Maine, 1838, 57-58, in Thornton's *Ancient Pemaquid.* Me. Hist. Soc., vol. 5, pp. 188-189.

higgen."[67] He later, however, locates "Munhiggen" as the place where he had been.

"And whither (I) myself was imployed by our Governor, with orders to take up such victuals as the ships could spare. Where I found kind entertainment and good respect, with a willingness to supply our wants. But, being not able to spare that quantity I required (by reason of the necessity of some among themselves whom they supplied before my coming), would not take any Bills (of Exchange) for the same: but did what they could freely, wishing their store had been such as they might in greater measure have expressed their own love, and supplied our necessities, for which they sorrowed, provoking one another to the utmost of their abilities. Which, although it were not much, amongst so many people as were at the Plantation, yet through the provident and discreet care of the Governors, recovered and preserved strength till our own crop on the ground was ready."

Winslow must have sent these supplies back by some boat, for he says: "Having dispatched there; I returned home with all speed convenient."

[67] Winslow, *Good News from New England* (1624).

CHAPTER XIII

WITH new blood in the Council of Plymouth, with men of rank and wealth sitting in the saddle, although twenty of them seem to have been chilled, through the controversy with the Virginia Colony, the portioning off of the land was made, to the twenty remaining. John Smith avers that they used his map, but either it was another apportionment that he was speaking of, or he was mistaken. The map has come down to us in two ways: First it was published in Purchas, *His Pilgrims*, in 1625, and later it is called Sir William Alexander's map and is published in his biography. A glance at the map, which is on page 162, will show that it was not Smith's map that was used, but probably Champlain's, or another French map.

While the Council was busy with these affairs, Sir William Alexander, a canny Scot, had not only obtained Nova Scotia, but was casting covetous eyes on the territory between the Penobscot and the Kennebec Rivers. This he afterwards obtained.

We have some fragments of the records of the meeting of the Council of New England.

There is a record of the Council for July 24, 1622, as follows:

"The Earle of Arundle to have for his devident, from the middle of Sagadahoc, and to goe North east soe much on his side as Mr Secretary goes on ye other side upon ye Coast. And to reach miles backward into ye Mayne, and 3 Leagues into ye Sea. And to have further into his Divident ye island called Menehigan.

"The Earle of Arundell — Sir Ferd. Gorges
Mr. Secretary Calvert — Sr Sam^{ll} Argall."

There is also a statement of the territory that is to belong to the Earl of Arundell made on the same day, for we find the following:

"24 July, 1622

"The Earle of Arrundle's Devid^{t}

The Earle of Arundell to have for a part of his divident from ye southermost poynt of Pershippscott East 12 Miles in a straight Lyne as the coast lyeth on ye Sea shoare. And 30 Miles by all that breadth upp into the Mayne Land due North, accompting 1760 yards to every Mile, with all ye fishings, Havens, Islands etc, lyeing as being

within 9 miles directly into
the Sea etc. Together with
ye Island of Menehiggan
etc, All lyeing betweene
the Degrees of 43 & 44."

The Council record of October 28 gives some light on the fishing privileges that caused so much trouble; it is given here in full:

"The Council Record of Monday 28°, Octo^r 1622.
"Dr. Barnabe Goche Treas
Sr Ferdinando Gorges Knt.
Sr Sam^ll Argall, Knt.

Atty^e Trēa^rs
Chamber

"It was proposed, what course should bee fittest to bee taken with these shipps that intend to goe in a fishing voyage for New England this yeare.

"1. It was thought fitt to demand from them five fishes out of every hundred. This to bee taken only of ye English Nation.

"2. Noe Stranger to bee allowed or suffered to fish there, That is to make dry fish. The reason, because that makeing of dry fish hath only been peculiar to Englishmen. And the Hollanders and Frenchmen only corre fish. If they should bee suffered to make dry fish, they would overlay it, and over throw the whole Trayd. For the debarring of Strangers, the mantaining of y^e Trade only to

MAP PUBLISHED BY PURCHAS, FOURTH VOLUME, 1625. ALSO CALLED SIR WILLIAM ALEXANDER'S MAP AND PUBLISHED IN "ENCOURAGEMENT TO COLONIES," 1630

The map was evidently made in 1623 from the Records of the New England Council as the property division shown corresponds to their records at that time

our owne people, Keeps still the Knowledge of makeing dry fish for England's Commonwealth."[68]

From this account it can be readily seen that Monhegan's isolation was an asset to the early Second Colony, and may perhaps be the reason why Gorges and some other writers of the time did not mention her by name. It was a safe place to dry fish and to keep the secret of the process for the English nation.

One record there is, of a meeting on the 28th of January, 1623, which is of interest to the history of Monhegan, and which has been preserved to us:[69]

"Tuesday ye 28th of Jan., 1623.

"The Lord Gorges — Sr Henry Spilman

Mr. Trear. — Sr Sam[ll] Argall

Sir Fer[d] Gorges

Com[s] for

Mennahigan

Sealed

The Com[s] for seizing of ye Island of Mannahigan is this day sealed and signed by ye Lord Duke of Lenox, the Lord Marquess Hamilton, the Earle of Arundle, the Earle of Holdernes, the Lord Georges, S[r] Robert

[68] Am. Antiq. Soc. Coll., 1867.

[69] Am. Antiq. Soc. Proc., April 24, 1867.

Mansell, Sr Fer^d Gorges,
Docter Matt:
Sutcleffe and
Mr. Trear."

This record of the meeting is in accord with the territory assigned to Arundell on Alexander's map, and it was undoubtedly given to him.

The Earl of Arundell was a connoisseur. He collected ancient objects of art and had exceedingly good taste. It is quite within his character to have selected Monhegan as his part of the territory, as it was at that time a very flourishing community, the foremost in the New England territory.

There does not seem to be any record of Jennens obtaining the island through grant from the Council, although there is a record of his having obtained land near Cape Cod on the mainland, where his name appears on the map as Mr. Ienigs. On account of missing records of the Council, historians have made the statement that he obtained it when he obtained his mainland grant. This is evidently an error. He was not of sufficient importance to have gotten it away from such a high-ranking person as the Earl of Arundell, and it will probably be found later, that either he or the Earl of Warwick, who was his employer, obtained the island from Arundell. But Arundell's grant did not obtain long, for Sir William Alexander, Earle of Starlinge, finally obtained Monhegan along with the other territory on the mainland.

Before Alexander obtained it, however, there was a redistribution of the plots of the territory by means of a high-grade lottery held on June 29, 1623:

"Sondaie 29° Junij 1623

"Att Greenwich

"There were presented to the Kings most excellent Matie a Plott of all the coasts and lands of New England, devided into twenty parts each part conteyning two shares, And twenty lotts conteyning the said double shares made up in little bales of waxe, And the names of twenty Patentees by whom these lotts were to be drawne. And for that the Lord Duke of Buckingham was then absent, his Matie was gratiously pleased to drawe the first lott in his Graces behalf, which conteyned the right number or share."

From July 24, 1622, Monhegan was no longer under the kindly authority of Gorges, whose "divident" lay on the mainland further down the coast. How the Island came to belong to Abraham Jennens, or Jennings, a prominent merchant extensively engaged in the fishing industry — owner of many fishing vessels, and a member of the Second Colony, and one of the Patentees of Newfoundland — is still a mystery. He may have drawn it in the lottery as he drew lot 5. At any rate, he obtained the Island about 1622, and continued and extended the trading post here, supplying the struggling plantations along the coast and the fishermen.

To this establishment for trading came many voyagers.

Mr. Thomas Weston, a merchant, shipowner, and financier of the Pilgrims, obtained a charter for a colony in New England. The first members of this colony, which was located near the Pilgrims at Wessagusett (Weymouth), consisted of fifty or sixty worthless fellows, under an overseer by the name of John Sanders. They are reported, by the pious Pilgrims, as being a profligate crowd, and soon used up their provisions, got in trouble with the Indians, and Myles Standish was sent to help them out. There is one report that Standish supplied them with provisions and accompanied them to Monhegan, where they hoped to meet Weston, but it appears probable that they came in their own small boat, the *Swan*. What became of them after they reached Monhegan is not now known. They may have scattered; some returning to England on the fishing vessels, others remaining to become a part of the troublesome renegades that thronged the coast later.

Although the Island of Monhegan belonged to Abraham Jennens, he seems to have had associated with him in trading his brother Ambrose and William Cross, a merchant of Plymouth, at least during June and July of 1624. Their factors, or traders, stationed that season on Monhegan were: Thomas Piddock, Edmund Dockett and William Pomfret, a distiller. With three traders for furs and fish the place must have been a very busy one, and perhaps a merry one, in 1624.[70]

[70] Bolton, *The Real Founders of New England.*

MONHEGAN

Phinehas Pratt's Narrative speaks of Munhigin and also of an Indian "caled Rumhigin who undertook to pilot a boat to Plimoth but that all lost their lives."[71]

There is also a record of another person on the Island this year:

"William Vengham, planted upon that island (Monhegan) June-July 1624, A man of experience in those parts."[72]

Christopher Levett, one of the Council for New England, obtained a grant of 6,000 acres of land in the Company's territory, in 1623, for £110 sterling, and has left a most valuable and interesting account of his voyage of 1623-24.[73]

He roamed the coast in a small boat, met Samoset[74] and has this to say of him:

"Somerset, a sagamore, one that hath been found very faithful to the English, and hath saved the lives of many of our nation, some from starving, others from killing.

[71] *Mass. Hist. Soc. Coll.*, ser. IV, vol. 4, p. 475.

[72] Putnam's *Gen. Mag.*, Dec., 1916.

[73] *Me. Hist. Soc. Coll.*, vol. 2, pp. 75-110.

[74] Samoset belonged to the Abenaki tribe of Indians that were located in the Maine territory and was a sagamore of one of the tribes of the Bashabes of the Penobscot. The history, origin and legends of this tribe are exceedingly interesting and should anyone wish to follow them to a later period, there is a delightful story written by Kenneth Roberts, *Arundel*, which gives a very vivid picture of their kindliness, and of their customs, and habits, at the time Arnold marched to Quebec. This tribe never acknowledged any Indian ancestry.

"And Somerset told that his son was born whilst I was in the country, and whome he would needs have to name and mine should be brothers and that there should be *mouchicke legamatch*[75] (that is friendship) betwixt them until Tanto carried them to his wigwam, (that is until they died.)" Levett says that *mouchicke* is a word of great weight, he also tells of the products of the country:

"There is great store of parsley, and divers other wholesome herbs, both for profit and pleasure, with great store of sassafras, sarsaparilla and aniseeds."

Having been told that Pemaquid, Capmanwagan and Monhiggon were granted to others he established himself at Quack, which he named York.

Other traders, also, came to the trading post at Monhegan. We have two records of such visits:

"Isaac Allerton, of Plymouth, N. E., and one of the first of the settlers there in 1625, originally opened and commenced the trade with our Eastern neighbors. By a little barter from year to year at Monhegan and the vicinity, etc."

"Plymouth colonists had made coasting trips to the eastward to obtain necessary supplies from the fishing ships at Monhegan, and learned of the furs which the natives brought to the mouth of the Kenebec, and coveted that trade."

The Jennens firm decided to sell their holdings, in

[75] Captain Smith gives the meaning of the Indian words "*Mawchick Chammy*, the best of friends."

1626, and we have the statement of Bradford as to the stock of goods and other commodities that they had at the trading post at that time:

". . . and wanting trading goods, they understood that a plantation which was at Monhegan, and belonged to some merchants of Plimoth was to brake up, and diverse usefull goods was ther to be sould; the Gove[r] and Mr. Winslow tooke a boat and some hands and went thither. But Mr. David Thomson, who lived at Pascataway, understanding their purpose, tooke opportunitie to goe with them, which was some hinderence to them both; for they perceiveing their joynt desires to buy, held their goods at higher rates; and not only so, but would not sell a parcell of their trading goods, excepte thay sould all. So, lest they should further prejudice one an other, they agreed to buy all, and devid them equally between them. They bought allso a parcell of goats, which they distributed at home as they saw neede and occasion, and tooke corne for them of the people, which gave them good content. Their moyety of the goods came to above 400 li starling. Ther was allso that spring a French ship cast away at Sagadahock, in which were many Biscaie ruggs and other commodities, which were falen into these mens hands, and some other fishermen at Damarinscove, which were allso bought in partnership and made their part arise to above 500 li. This they made shift to pay for, for the most part, with the beaver and commodities they had gott the winter before, and what they had gathered up that somer. Mr.

Thomson having some thing overcharged himselfe, desired they would take some of his, but they refused except that he would let them have his French goods only; and the marchant (who was one of Bristol) would take their bill for to be paid the next year. They were both willing, so they became ingaged for them and tooke them. By which means they became very well furnished for trade. . . ."

But Jennens also wanted to sell Monhegan Island. Two merchants of Bristol, Abraham Aldworth and Gyles Elbridge, who had been members of the Second Colony, and always interested in New England, hearing of this, arranged to send over their trusted man, Abraham Shurt, to buy the Island for them.

At this time land could not be conveyed legally through papers only, or away from the premises to be conveyed. It had to be seized through a ritual of "twig and turf," that is, some actual earth from the property and a twig from a bush or tree had literally to change hands.[76] Evidently this formality had not taken place at Monhegan before, or if it had we do not now have the record.

Sullivan, the earliest Maine historian, says:

"Monhegan Island was sold by Mr. Jennings of Plimouth, to Abraham Adlwarth & Mr. Gyles Elbridge, March 6, 1626, and improved ever since till the war of 1688."

[76] This information was given me by the present State Historian of Maine, Mr. Libby, and is also found in Johnston's *Bristol, Bremen and Pemaquid.*

We also have a statement by Shurt:

". . . in the year 1626, alderman Alsworth, Mr. Gyles Elbridge of Bristol, Merchants. sent over this Deponent for their Agent. and gave Power to him to buy Monhegan, which then belonged to Mr. Abraham Jennings of Plimoth, who they understood was willing to sell it, and having Conference with their Agent, about the price therof, agreed for fifty Pounds, and the Pattent to be delivered up: and gave him a bill upon Alderman Alsworth; which bill being presented, was paid as the Aforesaid wrote me."

This is probably the earliest bill of exchange mentioned in our commercial history.

CHAPTER XIV

MONHEGAN now came under the benign influence and personal administration of Shurt, who resided here for two or three years, and it undoubtedly flourished. John Brown, probably from Monhegan, obtained a portion of land at New Harbor from Samrset, which Samoset signed with a bow, as his mark, and which was later certified by

Shurt. Little by little plots of ground were obtained in this way on the mainland, opposite Monhegan, and Aldworth and Elbridge, or Shurt, as their agent, on the removal of their people to these places, fortified the southern point of the mouth of the Pemaquid River. Feeling it wise and necessary to enlarge their possessions, or to get proper authority, Aldworth and Elbridge asked for and obtained a grant of land, in 1631, on the mainland opposite Monhegan from the Council of New England:

"12,000 acres of land where the people or servants of the said Robert Aldworth and Gyles Elbridge are now settled, or have inhabited for the space of three years last past."

The delivery of the title to this land appears to have reached Shurt in 1633 and so headquarters were removed, then or before, from Monhegan. Under this grant the patentees were under obligation to nurture a settlement on the 12,000 acres. Belonging to the same people, Monhegan now loses her identity as a unit and becomes a part of the Pemaquid holdings.

Discontented people in England were becoming more and more interested in New England as a refuge from the religious troubles of the time and because of their desire for a greater opportunity and freedom. Some merchants of Dorchester, who had become interested in the trade in fish and furs in New England, applied to the Council of New England for a charter. This they obtained in 1629 under the name of "The Colony of Massachusetts Bay." These people were later called "The Puritans." They became the dominating influence, the controlling and governing force which really established order in New England, and it is mainly to their stalwart efforts that America became independent later.

Thomas Elbridge, after Aldworth's death, and also that of his father and elder brother, obtained possession of the patent to the Pemaquid territory, for we have an affidavit by Shurt:

"About 1629 Mr. Thomas Elbridge coming to Pemaquid, to whom the patent by possession did belong, and appertain, called a court, unto which divers of the then inhabitants of Monhegan and Damariscove repaired, and continued their fishing, paying a certain acknowledgement.

"Sworn by Abram Shurt Before Richard Russell, 1662."

From Sil. (Sylvanus) Davis' Report (1675):

"Thomas Elbridge, the son of Giles, the patentee, came over a few years afterward and held a court within this patent (Pemaquid Patent), to which many of the inhabitants of Monhegan and Damariscove repaired, and made acknowledgment of submission."[77]

There is a record that John Parker, mate of the *Mayflower* in 1620, was fishing at Monhegan in 1629.[78]

By this time there must have been a large community living on Monhegan. They must have had log houses, chinked with moss or clay, with thatched roofs. These were undoubtedly of the simplest construction. A large rectangular room, one story high, with a loft overhead which extended over a large part of the room, and reached by stairs or a ladder. They may even have had rough partitions both in the loft and the lower floor. The floors were either of split logs or of packed earth or clay. The fireplace was made of rough stones, and the chimneys of boards or short sticks crossing each other and plastered inside with clay.

But affairs in England were in a turmoil. King James of England had been very anxious to arrange a marriage between his son, Prince Charles, and Maria, the sister of

[77] *Me. Hist. Soc. Coll.*, vol. 1, p. 40.

[78] *Me. Hist. Soc. Coll.*, vol. 2, p. 192.

Philip IV of Spain. The young Prince had been sent to Spain with his evil genius, Buckingham, to court the young Princess Maria. On his way home Buckingham, who had been offensive at the Spanish Court, arranged for Prince Charles to visit Paris *incognito*. Here Charles met the Princess Henrietta, decided he liked her better than Maria, and so broke off his marriage to the Spanish princess. This treatment of his sister caused Philip IV to threaten war with England.

King James died suddenly, in March of 1625, and Charles I came to the throne. He then proceeded to marry Henrietta, and with her advent, the French gained enough influence to have their twice ravaged territory in Canada restored to them, and Catholicism regained some of its lost ground. Sir David Kirke had, on two separate expeditions, in 1627 and again in 1629, destroyed the French settlements in Canada and had brought home with him the Governor, Sieur de Champlain, as a prisoner of war. But the war with Spain and France ended in 1629 just as Kirke got home. By the Treaty of St. Germaine, in 1632, England conceded to France the title to Acadia and also Nova Scotia. The French immediately began to restore their settlements, and Razilly, with his lieutenant D'Aulnay, was put in command of all the territory west of the St. Croix River; De La Tour was commandant of all to the east of it. These two Frenchmen became rivals in the trade with the Indians, got into trouble with the Massachusetts colonists and pillaged each other's trading posts and were considered dangerous neighbors for the little settlement such as Monhegan now was. They ranged the coasts, disregarded the claims of the English merchants,

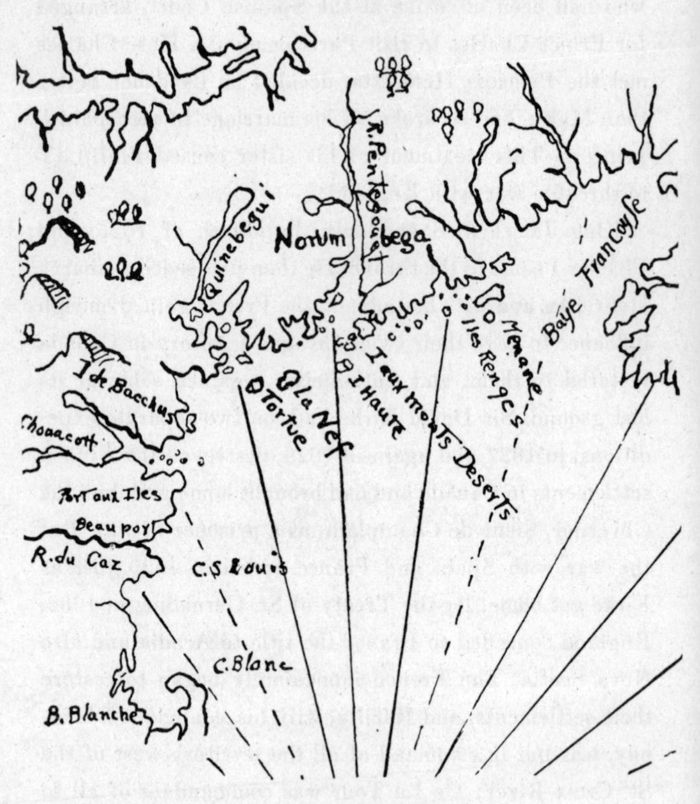

TRACING OF PORTION OF FRENCH MAP IN JOHN DE LAET'S "NOVIS ORBIS AMERIC," 1633

New York Public Library. This map maker evidently thought Champlain named Monhegan Tortue on one voyage

who had little trading settlements on the Penobscot and Kennebec, captured vessels, and were generally feared. De La Tour was an acquaintance and friend of Sir William Alexander, and was also friendly with the Massachusetts Bay colonists.

The French D'Aulnay robbed the Penobscot trading post of the Bay Colony of its contents, coats, rugs, blankets and bread, the usual assortment for Indian traffic. At about the same time they captured Dixy Bull, whom they caught trading within their territory.

"Then Bull took to himself a company of desperadoes and raised the black flag of piracy, which now for the first time, waved on the coast of New England. They took several vessels at sea, and rifled the fort at Pemaquid, and plundered the planters. As they were weighing anchor, one of the leaders was disposed of by a well aimed ball from a musket in the hands of one of Shurt's men on the shore. Fear seized on some of the less hardened, the crew was weakened by desertion, and the more desperate fled to the eastward."

Shurt by his uniform square dealing had secured the good will of the natives, and their trade; he kept the peace with both D'Aulnay and De La Tour, and even the members of the rival Colony of Massachusetts Bay seem to have valued his friendship. Thornton says that D'Aulnay was in debt to Shurt.

"More than enough of the refuse and scum of the world always drifts around border life, and Pemaquid with her sister colonists, was not exempt from this evil. From Weston's notable importation of vagabonds, alone, the buccaneer could whistle to his decks whole crews of graceless followers. Allerton, a renegade from Plymouth, early in this year, 'set up a company of base fellows, and made them traders,' along the coast at the Kennebec, Penobscot, Machias, and wherever they could barter."[79]

We know that Allerton was at Monhegan in 1626 and it is quite probable that there were many of the dissolute fellows in and about Monhegan.

It was, probably, for these reasons, the sagacious Shurt withdrew the little colony that was on Monhegan to his fortified position at Pemaquid.

Richard Mathers, on his way from England to Massachusetts, says in his Journal, under date of August 7, 1635, "that they made Menhiggen, an island without inhabitants."

Again we have Bradford's Journal giving an incident that took place on Monhegan in 1641, which would indicate that the Island is still without inhabitants:[80]

". . . 'about the beginning of the frost,' when a shallop

[79] Thornton, *Ancient Pemaquid*, p. 204.

[80] From "Something About Monhegan," E. H. Goss, *Mag. of Am. Hist.*, vol. 12, p. 266.

with eight men started from Piscataqua for Pemaquid, 'they would needs set forth upon the Lord's day, though forewarned.' A northeast storm arose, which drove them out to sea, and after fourteen days of suffering and trial, they reached Monhegan. Four of them died from exposure to the cold, and the remaining four were rescued by a fisherman, who discovered them in their famished condition."

On May 29, 1643, the colonists in Massachusetts, Plymouth, Connecticut and New Haven entered into a confederation for mutual protection from their hostile neighbors, the Indians, and the Dutch in New York, and other enemies at home. This confederation was called "The United Colonies of New England," and lasted for forty years. It was conducive of much benefit to the growing needs of the young settlements.

But the fishermen were using the houses and flaking stages on Monhegan every summer, for we have enough records of troubles, that had to be settled by law, to prove this.

Paul Mansfield, in 1644, sent freight of fish from Monhegan to Marblehead by Andrew Woodbery, who had to sue him for his pay; this he recovered eight years later, in 1652.[81]

Fishermen were at Monhegan in 1647[82] and in 1648[83] Ipswich fishing vessels fished here all summer.

[81] *Essex Court Records*, III, p. 14.

[82] *Suffolk Deeds*, III, p. 100.

[83] Hubbard, *General Hist. of N. E.*, p. 532.

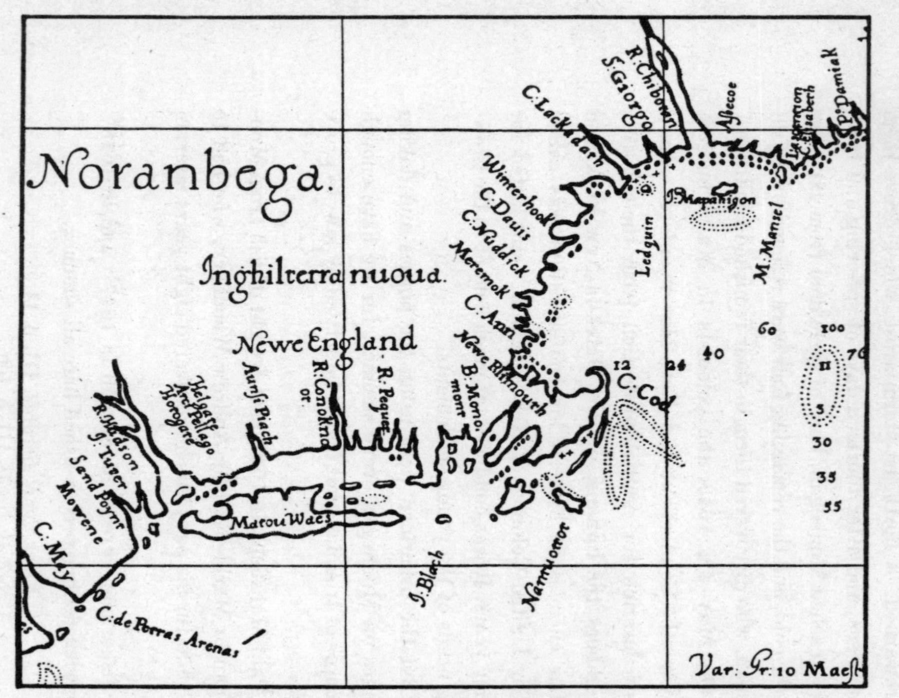

MAP OF LUCINI FECA IN "DELL ARCANO DEL MARE" BY DUDLEY IN 1646

Monhegan called Mapahigon is greatly exaggerated in size, showing

The Council for New England were having desperate troubles in the meantime, and Gorges and his associates were forced by the King to give up a very large part of their territory to Sir William Alexander's son, William Alexander, Lord Alexander. At first the grant did not include the immediate territory of Pemaquid, but at the last meeting of the Council this small part was, under date of November 1, 1638, included. This grant by the King to the Alexanders included Long Island, in New York, which was named Isle of Starlinge, so Monhegan now became a part of New Scotland. Sir William Alexander's scheme of colonization of this vast territory was to create an Order of Knights Baronets (hereditary), the word Sir to be prefixed to their proper name and the style and title of Baronet subjoined to their surnames, and that of "Ladie, Madame, and Dame" was to be prefixed to the names of their wives. By this means Sir William hoped to finance his scheme and to give importance and dignity to the undertaking.

The Baronets were to pay Sir William 1,000 merks Scottish money, for his past charges and for resigning to them his interest in the lands (10,000 acres) included in the barony. They were also to send out, each of them, a colony of six men, armed, appareled and victualled for two years. But they were allowed to commute for sending the six men by the payment of 2,000 merks, which was to be applied in furtherance of colonization in New Scotland. The lands were first resigned to the King, and by him regranted to the several Knights Baronets.

Alexander's son died in 1638, before the scheme got under much headway, and it languished somewhat. At any rate, we find that Henry, fourth Earl of Stirling, sold this grant to the Duke of York in 1663.

During the period of thirty-odd years, if any of the Baronets settled inside or outside the Pemaquid holdings or ever reached Monhegan, and if the owners of Monhegan and Pemaquid paid any part toward the scheme, no records are at this time available. Nevertheless, Sir William Alexander's authority over the Aldworth-Elbridge territory superceded that of the Council for New England, and lasted for the thirty-odd years as part of New Scotland, during that most turbulent time in English history, when the weak Charles I was on the throne. Charles had promised the Pope to establish Catholicism in New England.

Charles I was beheaded in 1649, and the Revolution and the establishment of an English Republic deterred new colonists from coming to New England, while religious differences waxed furious in Europe. This trouble in England left the colonists at loose ends, but allowed the lusty infants a chance to grow and to become like all young things, independent.

Thomas Elbridge was evidently a poor financier for we find that he had to mortgage Monhegan, in 1650, to Abraham Shurt for we have the record:

"10 (10) 1650 Thomas Elbridge of Pemaquid in N. E. Merch' granted vnto Abraham Shurt the Island of Monhigan in New England. wth all the houses edifices buildings woods vnderwoods commons meadowes pastures feedings & commodities there to appertaineing. wth pfitts issues due & payable vpon any demise or lease thereof or any pt there of reserved, wth all evidences concerning the same: Provided that if the sd Tho. Elbridge shall pay or cause to be pd vnto sd Abraham Shurt or his assigns the summe of thirty pounds sterl^g at or before the 29th of Sept. 1651, that then this grant shal be void. dat^d 11th Sept. 1650.

"Thomas Elbridge & a seale

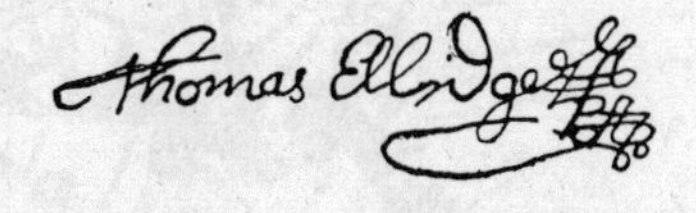

"Sealed and dd in pnce of
John Daud
Robert Long

"This deed was affirmed by Mr John Daud of Boston to be signed sealed and dd by m^r Tho. Elbridge to m^r Abr. Shurt his vse. before me

"William Hibbins:"[84]

There are several conflicting statements of Elbridge's transactions at this time.

According to J. W. Porter, in *Island of Monhegan*, in February 5, 1652, Elbridge sold one-half of his interest to Richard Russell of Charlestown, Mass., and on May

[84] *Suffolk Deeds*, Liber I, p. 131.

THE DANCKER'S MAP

From Stokes *Iconographie of Manhattan Island*, 1651-55

27, 1653, the other half to Nicholson Davidson of Charlestown, Mass. In July of 1657 Russell sold out his half to Davidson. While Mr. Charles Francis Jenney, in *The Fortunate Island of Monhegan*, says that Thomas Elbridge by two deeds, one dated April 14, 1657, the other dated September 3, 1657, conveyed the Island to Nicholas Davidson, a merchant of Charlestown, Mass., who about the same time, July 21, 1657, took an assignment of the mortgage to Richard Russell. The consideration of these deeds was eighty-five pounds, but the conveyance included a moiety of the entire Pemaquid Patent.

While the date is uncertain the facts are that Davidson became the owner. Under this ownership, of Davidson and his heirs, which lasted about ninety years, the Island became populated with splendid specimens of colonists.

CHAPTER XV

CROMWELL became dictator of England, and, being a friend to the Massachusetts Bay Colony, sent over two commissioners, Robert Sedgwick and John Leverett, to oust the Dutch from New York. But the news coming of a peace with the Netherlands, prevented the carrying out of this plan. Sedgwick, the Commander-in-Chief, then joined forces with Massachusetts for a campaign against the French forts in Acadia and Nova Scotia. These they succeeded in capturing. This happening in 1654, cleared the way for the inhabiting of Monhegan again by the fishing fraternity.

The Massachusetts Bay Colony merchants, having trading stations on the Penobscot and the Kennebec, knew Shurt, Elbridge, and Davidson, and their ships must have often passed and repassed Monhegan in their voyages to and fro. How they came to establish their authority over the Pemaquid territory will be told later. That Boston fishermen used Monhegan as a post is certain, for from the Records of the Court of Assistants of the Colony of the Massachusetts Bay, 1630-1692, we have the fragments of the records of a trial for murder committed on Monhegan in 1654, by Boston fishermen.

The story is briefly: A bark belonging to Nathaniel and Samuel Gallop was on a fishing voyage to Monhegan from

January to November of 1654. The bark was commanded by Matthew Kehnige, or Cemidge, or Keninge. The fishermen were all young men of twenty-six or twenty-seven years of age. John Short and Gregory Castle, or Cassell, were the boat's crew, John Barker or Baster, was the headman or shoreman. Other members of the bark's crew seem to have been Thomas Mitchell and Peter Warren. Whether the owners were along or not does not appear to be clear in the scanty record.

Castle was a drinking man and quarrelsome. He evidently disliked the master, Keninge, and always sought a quarrel with him on the slightest provocation. One day, as Keninge was sitting outside his house mending his shoes, Castle came along and took his hammer, and then struck him on the head with it. Keninge was badly hurt, although he seems to have continued to try to attend to his duties. After some little time, he finally died from the injury, and Castle was taken to Boston to stand trial. How it came out is not known, but he was probably dealt with according to his crime, as Peter Warren was an eyewitness to the assault.

That other fishermen used the Island during this time we know, for, in 1650, Valentine Hill made a voyage to Monhegan, and had litigation about it with one of his men. At least one of his crew remained on the island. In the same year John Devouex left two swine on the island.[85]

[85] *Essex Court Records,* I, pp. 214-216, 325.

Edward Hilliard, in 1654, brought suit against John Ridgway for "freight of fish from Monhegan to Charlestowne."[86] Apparently he met with success in his suit, or other creditors pursued Ridgway, for, in the next year, he tendered to his creditors among other things, "two bills with men's hands to them y^t then (as It seemed to them) did liue at Monhegan."[87]

General Monk restored the Stuarts to the English throne in the person of Charles II, in 1660, and his brother, the Duke of York, in 1663, bought out the interest in the land between the Kennebec and the St. Croix River, of which Monhegan was then a part, from Henry, 4th Earl of Stirling, who had derived his title from the Patent issued to Sir William Alexander, the first Earl, by the Great Council of New England in 1634, as we have noted before. To enlarge this grant Charles II bestowed upon the Duke of York, James Stuart, his brother, the territories of the New Netherlands, as the Dutch possessions at New York were called, and Sagadahoc. This Royal Charter also confirmed his title to the land he had bought from the Earl of Stirling.

After the Duke of York had purchased his territory, and obtained his grant from his brother, he set up a government at New York in 1665. Three royal commissioners from the Duke's government visited Pemaquid and established a county, which they called "Cornwall"; they ap-

[86] *Essex Court Records*, I, p. 325.
[87] *Suffolk Deeds*, II, p. 144.

pointed officers, and called on the inhabitants to appear and take the oath of allegiance. No inhabitant of Monhegan went to take the oath. The Commissioners also made peace with the Indians, built Fort George and garrisoned it, established a customhouse, made regulations for trading with the Indians, and set up the Duke's ownership of the soil, under the charter of Charles II, disregarding all prior patents, and required the settlers to pay a quit-rent of one shilling for each one hundred acres actually occupied or improved. For eight years after, however, they failed to pay any attention to the little settlements in Maine and affairs there, without government, became very desperate indeed. All sorts of malefactors, and renegades, settled and roamed the coast.

That John Dollen was on Monhegan in 1661 is certain, for we have the following information:

"Issigate, Indian, and Wombus, Indian, & Minicoate son to Issigate Deed to John Dallen of Monhegan two of the western Islands of St. Gorges, June 20, 1661. Assigned to John Foster & Wm. Hobby, 29 Feb, 1699."[88]

English fishermen were still coming for the fishing season, for we find that William Shackerly of Plymouth, Eng., was at Monhegan in 1661.[89]

John Josselyn, a relative of the famous old pioneer, Henry "Josselin," was here twice from England visiting. He wrote two books: one, an *Account of two Voyages*

[88] *Me. Hist. Soc. Coll. Doc. Hist.*, vol. 23.

[89] *Essex Court Records*, II, p. 313.

made to New England, 1638, 1663; the other, *New England Rareties.*[90]

From the former account there is a description of the fishing, a bit sad but possibly not untruthful:

"To every Shallop belong four fishermen, a Master or Steersman, a midship-man, and a Foremastman, and a shore man who washes it out of the salt, and dries it upon hurdles pitcht upon stakes breast high and tends their Cookery; these often get in one voyage Eight or Nine pounds a man for their shares, but it doth some of them little good, for the Merchant to increase his gains by putting off his Commodity in the midst of their voyages, and at the end thereof comes in with a walking Tavern, a Bark laden with the Legitimate bloud of the rich grape, which they bring from *Phial* (*Fayal*), *Madera, Canaries,* with *Brandy, Rhum,* the *Barbadoes strong-water,* and *Tobacco,* coming ashore he gives them a Taster or two, which so charms them, that for no perswasions that their imployers can use will they go out to Sea, although fair and seasonable weather, for two or three days, nay sometimes a whole week till they are wearied with drinking, taking ashore two or three Hogsheads of *Wine* and *Rhum* to drink off when the Merchant is gone. If a man of quality chance to come where they are roystering and gulling in *Wine* with a dear felicity, he must be sociable and *Roly-*

[90] *The New England Rareties* is about the herbs and flora of the country, which shows that the English are still interested in the drugs coming from the country formerly called "Drogeo."

poly with them, taking off their liberal cups as freely, or else be gone, which is best for him, for when *Wine* in the guts is at full Tide, they quarrel, fight and do one another mischief, which is the conclusion of their drunken compotations. When the day of payment comes, they may justly complain of their costly sin of drunkeness, for their shares will do no more than pay the reckoning; if they save a Kental or two to buy shooes and stockins, shirts and wastcoats with, 'tis well, other-wise they must enter into Merchants slaves, & when it riseth to a big sum are constrained to mortgage their plantation if they have any, the Merchant when the time is expired is sure to seize upon Their plantation and stock of Cattle, turning them out of house and home, poor Creatures, to look out for a new habitation in some remote place where they begin the world again."

But the French Catholics were still determined to retain their possessions in Canada and again on July 21, 1667, by the Treaty of Breda, Nova Scotia was restored to them. By this time the French Jesuits had made fast allies of the Indians, who considered the French superior to the English. It would require too much space to enter fully into this subject.

This period of our history was colored by the religious controversies between the Puritans, the weak Papist King Charles and the ambitious Louis XIV, also Catholic.

Another mention of John Dollen, the stalwart citizen of Monhegan, is made in 1669 when Thomas Elbridge,

"Gentleman of Aldertown in England," granted land at Round Pond to "John Dollen, fisherman of Mount Hegon."[91] This he sold in 1699 to John Foster and Wm. Hobby of Boston.[92]

Francis Johnson of Marblehead sued Richard Bedford, in 1672, for "damage on a fishing voyage at Monhegan," claiming that the defendant, a shoreman, who by his drunkenness and neglect caused injury to fish to the extent of about 30 £. The plaintiff's verdict was, "Damages to be paid in fish at Monhegan."[93] Bedford in turn sued Johnson and one Grant for injury caused by his loss of his "share and craft" in said voyage, and also had a verdict. There was evidence that Bedford refused to leave the Island with the company, "would make himself drunk, . . . would lie under the flakes or in one house or another and let the fish lie 'upon spoiles.' He would also get others to drink with him, with the bottle in the knee of his breeches." This same season, William Browne, Sr., bought fish from some fisherman at the Island.

Massachusetts was extending her authority more and more to her weaker neighbor, who had seemingly no authority to govern, and no other government, as the Duke of York's representative, in New York, ignored this part of his territories entirely.

George Munjoy, or Mountjoy, under the authority of

[91] *Suffolk Deeds*, LVII, p. 241.

[92] Johnston, *Bristol, Bremen and Pemaquid*, p. 233.

[93] *Essex Court Records*, VI.

an "Act of the Massachusetts Council," in 1671, surveyed the patent of the colony and made a report in 1672. He reported to the Council:

"If the honoured Court were pleased to goe twenty minitts more northerly in Merrimack Riuer it would take in the inhabitants and places East along & they seeme to much desire it."[94]

This took in Monhegan and Pemaquid, and most of Georges Island.

The Duke of York's representative in New York, probably hearing of Munjoy's line and of the popularity of the Massachusetts government in his territory, sent a letter from "Fort James on ye Island Manhatans in N: Yorke, ffeb: 16, 167⅔," asking "what kind of government the people wanted." It is addressed, "Lre to ye Inhabitants of Pemaquid." and signed by "Yo[r] Very Affectionate ffriend, Fran: Lovelace."[95]

In this same month the inhabitants, to show that they desired the government of Massachusetts to extend her wings over them, sent a petition under date of May 18, 1672:

"To the Honoured Governor, Deputy Governour, Majestrates & Deputies Assembled in the General Court now sitting in Boston this 18th day of May, 1672.

"The petition of . . . several of the inhabitants of the Eastern parts of New England, viz[t] Kenebeck, Cape Bon-

[94] Johnston, *Bristol, Bremen and Pemaquid*, p. 109.
[95] *Me. Hist. Soc. Coll.*, vol. 5, pp. 7-8.

awagen Damares Cove Shipscoate Pemaquid & Monhegan. . . .

"Humbly Sheweth that whereas the Providence of God hath stated our habitations into those parts wherein some times past we have had some kind of government settled amongst us; but for these Several years have not had any at all which is greatly to our Prejudice & damage having no way to Right ourselves upon any Account whatsoever & have little hopes of obtaining any to be helpfull to us for the good of our Soles, unless we have Government settled amongst us; The Humble Request therefore of your Petitioners is that you will please so farr to favour us as to take us under your Government and protection that we may all have the Benefit of all those Laws settled among yourselves granted unto us which if this Honourable Court shall accept of & granted to us we have desired our loveing friend Mr Richard Collecott to advise with this honoured Court or committee wh they shall appoint for that purpose, & so to act in our behalf what shall be Judged meet or conveinent for us whereby your Petitioners shall be ever Engaged to pray &c."

"(Signers)

"Kennebeck, 21 names.

"Shipscoate, 15 names.

"Cape Bonawagon, 16 names.

"Pemaquid, 11 names.

"Damaris Cove, 15 names.

"Monhegan:

MONHEGAN

Thornton[96]	*Porter*[97]	*Other Records.*
Jno Palmer	James Palmer,	
Jno Dollen,		Darling, Dalton, Dollin, Dollen, Dalling, Dolling,
Antho. Pedell,		Anthony Peadell.
Geo. Bickford,		
Reynold Celer,		Reynald Kelley, Kelly.
Jno Dare,		
Richd Woorring,	Richard Wooring,	
Edwd Dary,	Edward Davy,	
Thos Flewen,	Thomas Fleming,	
Richd Boone,	Richard Borne,	
Richd Oliver,		Olliuer, Olliver
Roger Willis,		
Hen. Stokes,		
Wm. Sanders,		
Robt Wittell,		
Abr^{m} Larkrow,	Abr'm Larkrau,	
Abel Horkridg,	Abel Harkridg,	Hoggeridge
Peter Widgor,	Peter Widger,	

These names are spelled as in Thornton excepting those noted.

"These were the names of the Persons Subscribers of the several Papers sent to Richd Collacott for Petition aforesaid."

Mr. Porter says: "The handwriting of these fishermen was not of the first order, and it is likely that the names would now be spelled much different."

From later records we find that Richard Patteshall owned a third of the meadow, along with John Palmer

[96] Thornton, *Ancient Pemaquid.*

[97] Porter, "Monhegan," *Bangor Hist. Mag.*, vol. 3, p. 141, 1888.

and John Dollen, and also "ASwamp lying on a hill above s^{d} Meadow Next to ye highway." Patteshall also had a stage and flaking privileges,[98] bought from Charles Harris, dated August 3, 1683.

If Charles Harris lived on the Island, as is inferred, his family would make the nineteenth one living here. From the Selectmen's records of Charlestown, Mass., there is a notation that Peter King arrived, with his wife and three children, at that town, October 21, 1689, from Monhegan. Here is a twentieth family. Then George Burnett was also a resident, for he was appointed one of the administrators of the estate of John Walter, a fisherman, who resided, on and off, on Monhegan. This would bring our count up to twenty-two. From this list of twenty-two families, surely Cadillac and Capt. Sylvanus Davis, who in a report dated 1701, estimated that there were "near" twenty fishing vessels at Monhegan, were well informed, as undoubtedly each family had, at least, one shallop.

Dollen's daughter was the wife of Reynold Kelly, one of the grand jurymen in 1674, according to a deed of 1717,[99] and as John Palmer, Sr., was authorized to marry persons, it is probable that he was the officiating magistrate on the occasion of their marriage, as Dollen had so long been a resident. Kelly owned land next to his father-in-law, but just which plot does not now appear.

[98] York Deeds, IX, p. 230; Sullivan, *History of Maine*, p. 162; Johnston, *Bristol, Bremen and Pemaquid*, p. 235.

[99] York Deeds, XVIII, p. 259. *Ibid.*, XIX, p. 67.

When John Palmer, Sr., went to Boston later he reported himself as being a carpenter. He must have built some of the houses then occupied by the residents. Skillful and industrious craftsmen were in abundance, on the coast, by this time, and building materials, owing to the establishment of the numerous sawmills on the rivers on the main, were of a higher type than formerly. They had bricks for their chimneys, as many of them have been uncovered in the old ruins, and cellars:

"The majority of the farmers and labourers, the common people of this period, had plain rectangular houses of one story, with two rooms, a kitchen or living room, and a family bed room, with one or more beds, and a trundel-bed."[100]

"The kitchen of this period was large, with an immense fireplace with its crane jack, spit and pot hooks. A Dutch oven was used for baking, covered with embers and later, potatoes were roasted in the hot ashes. Seats were placed in the chimney-corners for the children, and a high-backed settle for the elder people in front of the fire. Dipped candles and slivers of pitch pine, or candlewood, were used for lighting in the winter evenings.

"The principal articles of food in the earliest days was Indian corn. It was very productive, and was prepared in various ways. The Indians boiled it until it became tender, and ate it with fish and venison. They also parched it in hot ashes, then sifted it and pounded it into fine meal in

[100] Weeden, vol. 1, p. 212.

mortars, and ate it dry or mixed with water. The early settlers prepared it in the same way, made dough and baked it. They also soaked the corn, then pounded it in a mortar, boiled it, and ate it with milk, or butter and molasses; it was called samp. Indian meal or hasty pudding was made by boiling or baking the meal, and was eaten with milk or butter, and with molasses, as soon as this was obtained from the West Indies. Brown bread was made from a mixture of two parts of corn-meal with one part of rye. Succotash was made of beans boiled with corn in milk. Broth was made of the liquor of boiled salt meat and pork, mixed with meal. Bean porridge was made of beans boiled for a long time with salt beef or pork. Besides corn, in the early days, pork, poultry, fish, and wild game furnished food. Deer, wild turkeys, and pigeons were abundant. After a few years, a supply of meat from cattle was obtained.

"Home-brewed beer was universally used. It was made not only from barley but from Indian corn. The corn was sprouted, then washed and dried in a kiln, which made malt. Beer was also made from Indian corn bread, which was cut up and mashed, and used as malt. After 1650, cider was used more or less in place of beer.

"Broth, bean porridge, and hasty pudding and milk, furnished the usual evening and morning meal, and hasty pudding and milk, boiled salt pork and brown bread and cheese, the dinner. Neither coffee nor tea was used in that period."[101]

[101] Northend, *The Bay Colony.*

The petition made by the residents of Monhegan and other settlements was passed on favorably by the deputies, of the Massachusetts government, four days after its date (May 22), but was not confirmed by the magistrates, which included the Governor and Assistants. The subject, however, was again brought up before the General Court at its October session, in 1673, with a more favorable result.

Before final action was taken by either the government at New York, or by Massachusetts, the Dutch captured New York in 1673, and Lovelace fled to England. This cleared the way for the Massachusetts government to consider the "humble request" of the settlements, of which Monhegan was one. This action was taken at the General Court, held in Boston the 27th of May, 1674:

"In pursuance of an order of the General Court in Oct., 1673, it is ordered Major Thomas Clarke, Mr. Humphrey Davy, Mr. Richard Collecott, and Lieut. Thos. Gardiner, or any three of them, whereof Major Thomas Clark to be one, are fully empowred to repaire to Pemaquid, Capenwaghen, Kennebec, &c. or some one of them, to the eastward . . . to keep a County Court, to give oaths to the constables there appointed and to appoint meet persons, inhabitants there to offices and places within our patent."

This County Court of "Devon" was held July 22, 1674, at Pemaquid, and we have some records of the importance of the Monhegan men in affairs of that time:

"Richard Olliuer, of Monheghen, is nominated and appointed to be recorder and clarke of this county (Devon) and took oath accordingly."

And Jno Palmer, Sr., of Monhegan, was one of those:

". . . appoynted and Impowred by the Court as Commission^{rs} for ye yeare Ensuing and they or the Majo^{r} parte of them to hold & keep Commission^{rs} Courts in such places and as often as they shall see Cause within the County of Devon for ye Ending of Small cause, according to law, who alsoe haue magistraticall power in marrying such as are duly and legally published according to law, as a alsoe to punish Criminall offences according to the pticular Order of the General Court, Dated 27 May, 1674 in boston."

"Richard Olliver was chosen to be 'Clarke of Writs,' while John Dolling was to have liberty to keep a house of public entertainment and was to be given a permit to retail beer, wine and liquor for the next year."[102]

Richard Olliver seems to have had more education than most of the men of that time for he was made "Clarke of Writs," for the whole county as well as for the local court. John Palmer, Sr., was appointed to hold general court for small offences and could also marry people. So there must have been a number of women on the Island for a long time prior to 1674.

At this same time of oath taking, John Dolling took the oath of Constable. There were two grand jurymen from

[102] *Me. Hist. Soc. Doc. Hist.*, vol. 4, pp. 330, 344-5.

"Monheghen," George Bickford and Reynold Kelly. While Richard Olliver, Abel Haggeridg, Jn° Palmer, Senr and Jn° Palmer, Junr, Henry Stoakes, James Widger, Jn° Dare, John Dolling, Reynald Kelly, George Bickford, "tooke the oathe of fidelity."

At this same court the "administration of the eState of John Walter, a fisherman somtymes Resident of Monheghen & Sometymes of Damerells coue who dyed about four yeares since is granted to Geo. Burnett Resident at Monheghen who is to dispose of the same according to the cleerest testimony of and to whome ye estate doeth belong & to bring in an Inventory of the same to ye next comission court, heere & himselfe as principall and Richd Oliver as Suerty doe bind themselues in fifty pounds a peece that Order shall bee attended & B p formed."

At this same meeting was appointed:

"John Dolling, Sargeant & he to choose his Corporall there."

Monhegan, or "Monheghen," was taxed for the purposes of this same court and other expenses five pounds and ten shillings, showing that it had three times the wealth of Pemaquid, one pound more than any other single settlement, so it is readily seen that Monhegan was, even in 1672-74, the most flourishing settlement in the County of Devon, and so continued, as will be shown.

In the autumn of 1674 the General Court, by an act, authorized the Commissioners "to hear and determine all civil actions arising within the county to the value of ten pounds, any law, usage, or custom, to the contrary notwithstanding." This was done as it was thought it might be difficult to hold the whole Court of the County of Devon each year.

The following May the Commissioners appointed "associates for the county of Devonshire and to keepe courts for tenn pounds value, and either of them to take acknowledgment of deeds, marry such as are legally published, punish offenders, the penalty of which offences exceed not tenn shillings, or by whipping, not exceeding tenn stripes, and in other cases to bind them over to the associates and county courts."

No County courts seem to have been held in 1675, nor is there record of any held in 1676.

CHAPTER XVI

The Indians in this region, who had been for so many years friends of the English, gradually became debauched by the rival traders and their methods. These French, Dutch, and English merchants sold the Indians rum, often watering it; cheated them at every opportunity, sold them guns and ammunition, and taught the Indians how to use them. They became very often better marksmen than the pioneers. This period, of the Indian Wars, is a very dreadful chapter in American history.

Although the flame of hatred first started with Philip's War, in Massachusetts, on being quenched there, with the death of Philip, it broke out anew in Maine. The direct cause of the attack on Pemaquid and the neighboring settlements was the treachery of one Laughton, an inhabitant of Piscataqua, who, in the spring of 1676, enticed some Indians of Cape Sable, who were not in any way connected with the former outrages, on board his vessel and sold them into slavery.

The Indians along the coast did not really miss their comrades until later, when they commenced roaming up and down the seashore. Finally finding out that their comrades had been taken, they got into a violent rage and appealed to Mr. Earthy,[103] of Pemaquid, and Richard

[103] Mr. Earthy appears, from Hubbard's account, to have been

Oliver, of Monhegan, and others. These men could not believe the story true. However, it seems to have been so. The Indians, having been denied guns and shot, by the order of the Massachusetts authorities, and in consequence had gone hungry the winter before, now started out on the warpath in earnest. Mr. Earthy and Richard Oliver tried to make peace with them and went eastward to a conference of the tribes, but the fear-stricken inhabitants of the little settlements were so unruly that they could accomplish little in the way of a peace, although it was a heroic and noteworthy effort.

Hubbard, in his *Indian Wars in New England,*[104] tells of this most dreadful chapter in the history of these Maine settlements:

"But in the mean Time, such was the *Violence* used by some *refractory English* in those Parts, that they could scarce be *restrained* from *offering Violence* to the *Persons* he *sent up* as *Messengers,* or others that *lived quietly amongst them,* and did also as violently *set themselves* to oppose himself, or any others that acted with more *Moderation* then the Rest; protesting against them, as those who for Gain supplyed the Indians with Powder and shot, and said they would kill any Indian they met; others at Monhiggan offered *five* Pound for every Indian that should be brought, yet would not these Persons that were

either acting under Abraham Shurt, who must have been a very old man by this time, or to have been the agent of the owners of the Pemaquid and Monhegan territories.

[104] Hubbard, *Indian Wars in New England,* vol. 2, p. 152.

so violent against the Indians in the Discourse, be perswaded upon any Terms, then or afterward, to *go out to fight against* the Indians in an *orderly Way*: as appeared both by their Security in not *standing better* upon their Guard, and by their sudden Flight afterward, running away like a *Flock of Sheep*, at the *Barking* of any *little Dog*:"[105]

With the Indians burning, murdering and taking captives, the inhabitants of the Pemaquid holdings, and neighboring settlements, fled to Damariscove Island, and finally to Monhegan. Hubbard tells in detail of this flight, which occurred about the 20th of August, 1676:

"Upon ths report of this sad Disaster, all the Plantations of the English in those Parts, were soon left, and forsaken by Degrees. All the rest of the Inhabitants of Kennibeck River, Shipscot River, Sagadehock, Damanicottee, feering to be served in the same kind, fled to the Islands of Cape Bonawagan & Damorils Cove.

"On the *second Day at Night* a Post was sent to *Pemmaquid* to inform them of what had hapned, who being but *eight* or *ten Men*, were minded to go to the Island called Monhiggon, having secured the *best of their Goods*, but the wind taking them short, they were forced to turn into *Damorils Cove*, where they found Mr. *Wiswal* & Mr. *Colicot*. There they laboured *two Days* to settle a *Garrison*; But partly by the *Mutinousness* of the People, and partly by the *Want of Provision*, nothing could be done to

[105] Hubbard, *Indian Wars in New England*, vol. 2, p. 149.

secure the Island so that it was presently deserted: From thence they went to *Monhiggon,* resolving there to tarry till they had heard from *Boston,* from whence Mr. *Colicot* & Mr. *Wiswal* promised to their *utmost Endeavour* to send help. There they settled *three Guards,* and appointed *five & twenty to Watch every Night,* not knowing but that the Indians might come every Hour. But continuing ther a *Fort-night,* and finding no Relief like to come; & seeing all the Country *burned round about* (for after they had gotten all that could be saved from *Pemaquid,* they saw all the other Islands *Windgins, Corbins Sound, New Harbor, Pemaquid,* all on fire in two Hours time) then considering what was best to be done, they found no boats could be *sent to Sea* for fear of *weakening the Island,* & and most of those that were upon the Island, were *Strangers, Coasters,* & such as came from the *Mayne,* and were ready to be gone upon every Occasion, they laid an *Imbargoe* for one Weeks Time: after which a Letter was received from Major *Clark,* desiring their *Assistance* for enquiring after *Capt. Lake if alive,* saving what could be had at *Kennibeck,* &c. but intimating nothing of any Help like to come, besides those that *brought the Letter* told them, it was in *vain to expect* any Help from *Boston.* It being questioned there, what they had to do with those Parts, upon which the Inhabitants considered, that if they should tarry there, and spend all their *Provision,* & neither *be able* to go *to sea,* nor yet to *live,* or to be *safe ashore* for want of Help, it were better for them to remove, while they had something to *live upon*, & seek Imployment elsewhere; so by Consent they *resolved* forthwith to *transport themselves*, and what they *had saved* of their Goods to *some Place of Security*, so they took the *first Opportunity to set sayle*, some for Piscataqua, some for *Boston*, and some for *Salem*, at one of which *three* Places they all *safely arrived*."[106]

This narrative would seem to indicate that John Dollen had a considerable warehouse filled with provisions on Monhegan, at that time, or the people would not have gone there in their starving condition.

We know that there were three hundred people who took sanctuary on Damariscove Island;[107] that there were twenty families living on the Island; that there were about twenty fishing vessels whose home port was Monhegan, and also that there were many other vessels in the harbor; that at that time every fishing vessel had from four to five men attached to it. Roughly estimated, there must have been about five hundred people or more on Monhegan for that week or two of extreme terror. It certainly was fortunate that there was food for them in the larder. As Hubbard does not mention that they were without food, it is reasonable to suppose that they were properly fed. But there were forty of the people without guns and there was insufficient ammunition.[108] As Sergeant Dollen was

[106] Hubbard, *Indian Wars in New England*, vol. 2, p. 164.

[107] Johnston, *Bristol, Bremen and Pemaquid*, p. 126.

[108] *Me. Hist. Soc. Coll.*, 2nd ser., vol. 6, pp. 91, 118, 127.

probably in command, we can be sure that every precaution was taken for the safety of the assemblage, and that although they were crowded, none suffered privation.

The Duke of York's representative, learning of the plight of the inhabitants of the Pemaquid territory, acted promptly; as we have a record under date of September 8, 1676:

"Sept. 8, 1676:

"A Letter coming from Boston to the Governor from Mr Abr. Corbetts who lives to the Eastward, in the Dukes Patent, relateing the destruction of the Eastern parts near Pemaquid &c by ye Indians in the month of Aug^st^ last, about the 20th day of the month, The same being read and considered of.

"Resolved, to send a sloope to Piscâtaway Salem and Boston, to invite and bring as many of the Inhabitants particularly ffishermen as will come driven from the Dukes Territoryes, and parts Eastwards, and to supply them with Land in any part of the Government they shall chuse."[109]

The Massachusetts authorities, although a little tardy, still did take some action in regard to the outrages by the Indians; as will be seen from the following records of the General Court, October, 1676:

"It is hereby ordered, that, for the service in the eastern parts, there be twenty able souldjers, with twenty of

[109] "Papers Relating to Pemaquid," edited by Hough, in *Me. Hist. Soc. Coll.*, vol. 5, 1857.

our Indians, which shall be sent wth all expedition, fitted and furnished with arms, amunitions, & provisions sufficjent, in convenient vessells to Kinnibecke, Shipscott, Monhegin, & Casco Bay, or Black Point, or where they may have opportunity to doe service vpon the ennemy; and that Major^{r} Clarke be desired and is heereby authorized to rayse & send away sayd forces as abouesayd; and to put them vnder such conduct as himself, the council, or the General Court shall appoint."[110]

The Monhegan inhabitants stayed in their homes and went on with their peaceful labors. The Indians, although able to harass the mainland, because of their cleverness with their birch-bark canoes, were unable, at this time, to manage a sailing vessel or to cross the deep waters between Monhegan and the mainland, and so did not disturb the colony.

Richard Oliver, however, with Mr. Earthy, believing that Mugg, an Indian who had been with the English since he was a child, could manage a ransom for the captured inhabitants of the destroyed settlements on the mainland, and could negotiate a peace with the Indians Madockawando and Chebartina, "Sachems of Penobscot," went with Mugg to Boston on this errand. The Governor and Council of Massachusetts wrote the Articles of Peace, which included ransoming the English captives, which Mugg, who said that he would carry out the terms of the Treaty with his life, was to attempt to con-

[110] *Mass. Records,* vol. 5, p. 122.

summate. The Peace was signed by Richard Oliver, of Monhegan, and Mr. Earthy, of Pemaquid.

The story of Mugg's attempts is a long one, and as there were no prisoners from Monhegan, does not further enter into this history. Those who would wish to read the whole story will find it in Hubbard's *Indian Wars in New England,* vol. II.

By the action of the Duke of York's Council, June 9, 1677, that power decided to reassert its authority of the Pemaquid territory:

"All the ffishermen & old inhabitants to be restored and Protected."

Staunch John Dollen and the other residents having kept their possessions and domiciles intact, Monhegan was now the chief, as well as the strongest and most populous settlement on the seaboard.

When, therefore, the Duke's representative sent a garrison, with officers and soldiers to the fort at Pemaquid (Fort Charles), and established a local government, the Monhegan people were anxious to coöperate. They named Pemaquid "James Town," in honor of King James, and issued orders for the regulation of trade and affairs generally. The principal regulations were:

"The trading place to be at Pemaquid and no where else."

"All Entryes to bee made at New Yorke and no Coaster or Interlopers to be allowed, but if found to be made prise."

"Liberty of Stages upon the ffishing Islands but not upon the Maine, except at Pemaquid near the ffort."

"The Indyans not to goe to ye ffishing Islands."

"No rum to bee dranke on that side the ffort stands."

"No man to trust any Indyans."

"If Occasion one or more Constables to be appointed for the fishing Islands, and Indyans to have equall Justice and Dispatch."

"Fishermen to come to Pemaquid yearly to renew their Engagen[ts] and not to splitt or fling out their Gurry in the fishing grounds, or to trade with the Indyans to the prejudice of the fishery and hazard of these parts."

"Land to be given out indefferently to those that shall come and settle, but no trade to bee at any other place than Pemaquid, and none at all with the Indyans as formerly ordered."

"It shall not be Lawful for any Vessels Crew that belongeth not to the Government to make a voyage in the Government, except he hath a house or stage within the Government on penalty of forfeiture of paying for makeing his voyage."

"It shall not be Lawful for fishermen to keep any more dogges than one to a family on such penalty and forfeiture as shall be thought fitt by you (Capt. of the Fort)."

"No coasting vessel shall trade on the Coast as Bumboats tradeing from Harbor to Harbor, but shall supply the General account for one boate or more, neither shall it be lawful for him to trade in any other Harbor, but where the boat or boats are, neither, shall it be lawful fore him to trade with any other crew for Liquors or wine, Rumm, Beer, Sider, &c., on such penalty as you (Capt of Fort) think fitting."

"All vessels out of any Government if they come to trade and fish shall enter at Pemaquid, or the places appointed, and they shall not go in any other Harbor except by stress of weather."

"No stragling farmes shall be erected, nor no houses built any where under the number of twenty."

It can be readily seen that the Duke's government meant to punish the other New England colonies, especially that of Massachusetts, by excluding them from trade or fishing on the coast between the Kennebec and St. Croix Rivers; they also had in mind the French colonies.

As a result of these military operations and regulations the Indians soon came to terms and were persuaded to give up the English captives that they held and to restore the ketches that they had captured.

That Capt. Anthony Brockhole and Ensign Caesar Knapton were in earnest and prosecuted their orders is evident for several of the Boston traders had to go to New York to recover their vessels.[111]

Under this government John Dollen was willing to act as the Justice of the Peace. We have the first record of this:

[111] Johnston, *Bristol, Bremen and Pemaquid.*

"A Speciall Commission to the Court of Sessions att Pemaquid for the Tryall of Isreal Dymond and John Rashly About the Drowneing of Sam[ll] Collins."

This commission was composed of:

"John Joslyne Esq[r] Justice of the Peace in Quorum, Mr. John Dollen, Mr. Lawrence Dennis and Mr. John Jourdaine, Justices of the Peace."

Trade at Monhegan grew rapidly and they continued their fishing operations:

"In 1679 an enterprising trader by the name of Cox, a resident of Pemaquid but at that time at Piscataquid, wrote to Boston for a small loan to help fit out his vessel for Monhegan, where he hoped to exchange his commodities for furs, and thus make a profit."[112]

[112] Pattengill, *Monhegan, Historical and Picturesque.*

CHAPTER XVII

JOHN DOLLEN was again appointed Justice of the Peace in 1680, and he continued to hold that office, for we have a record of his reappointment for 1686. That law enforcement was necessary can be seen from the fact that in 1682 Richard Bass, an employee of Dollen, who is called Dalton in the report, ran away with Dollen's shallop, taking a servant of Dollen's and another resident of Monhegan with him. This resident is not given by name but is spoken of as "a liver in the place."[113]

In 1685 the Duke of York became James II, and all the American colonies were gradually gathered under the direct government of the English crown. Sir Edmond Andros was sent over as Governor General and had his headquarters in New York. John Palmer, not the John Palmer of Monhegan, but an Englishman bearing the same name, was appointed Deputy-Governor and stationed at Pemaquid by Governor Dongan at New York. From him several of the old residents of Monhegan obtained leases to their old homesteads. John Palmer, Sr., and John Dollen seem to have applied for new deeds. We have the record of the deed, given to John Dalling, as

[113] *Dukes County (Mass.) Deeds*, vol. 1, p. 283; *New England Hist. and Gen. Reg.*, vol. LII, p. 27; *Me. Hist. Soc. Coll.*, 2nd ser., vol. 4, p. 348.

he is here called. This elaborate paper[114] is given in full:

"John Palmer, Esq., one of the council in his Majestys Plantation and colony of New York and commissioner for the granting and confirming of lands within the County of Cornwell in the said colony,

"To all to whom these present shall come or may concern greeting. Know ye that by virtue of the Commission and authority unto me given by the right Honorable Colonel Thomas Dungan, lieutenant and gouvernour of the said colony, for and in behalf of our most gracious Sovereign lord James the Second, by the grace of God, of England, Scotland, France and Ireland, king, defender of the faith, Supreme lord of the plantation and colony aforesaid, I have given, granted, ratified and confirmed; and by these presents do give, grant, ratify and confirm unto John Dalling of Monhegan, in the county of Cornwell, yeoman, all that certain mesuage or tenement situate lying and being on the island of Monhegan, and whereon the said John Dalling now dwelleth: and singular the house, out houses, edifices, buildings, warehouses, barns, stables, orchards and way passages, water, water courses, lights, easements, profits, commodities, advantages, hereditaments and appurtenances whatso ever, occupied, possessed, or enjoyed, or attempted, deemed, and taken, as part or parcel or members thereof, or any part or parcel thereof, and also the several other parcels of land there now fenced or inclosed by the said John Dalling for

[114] Sullivan's *History of Maine.*

planting of Indian corn; with a full third part of a certain marsh or meadow, or the said island, and the stage and back room for the fishery there; with the liberty to fence in, and inclose any part or parcel of land on said island for his use and accommodation, not exceeding six acres. To have and to hold the said mesuage, or tenement, and all and singular other the premises, with their appurtenances, unto the said John Dalling, his heirs and assigns, to the sole and only proper use, benefit, and behalf of the said Dalling his heirs and assigns forever. *Yielding* and *paying therefor yearly and every year year unto* our *Sovereign lord and king, his heirs or* Successors, or to such governour or other officer as from time to time shall be by him or them appointed to receive the same on every twenty-fifth day of March forever, as a quit rent, or acknowledgment for the said land, one bushel of merchantable wheat, or the value thereof in money. In witness whereof I have hereunto set my hand and caused the Seal of the colony to be hereunto affixed, and these presents to be entered of record at James Town, the thirteenth day of September, in the Second year of his Majestys reign, Annoque Domini one thousand and six hundred and eighty six.

"J. Palmer

"Recorded the day of the date hereof

"John Velf, D. Secretary."

This deed gives a picture of the island, a bit faint but still interesting and authentic.

Dollen had fishing stands, probably boats to serve them, a dwelling house, or a house of entertainment, which was probably called an inn or tavern in those days. Meadows suggest live stock, fenced-in places suggest gardens and fields and considerable live stock on the Island. He had his gardens for growing Indian corn, and also fruit trees. These improvements take time and we may assume that he either bought from the earlier settlers their buildings and plots, or he had been for a long time on the Island even before our first record of 1661. He might even have been a descendant of Gorges' pioneers. That he was a middle-aged man of importance, with courage and good physique, is apparent from his being chosen "Sergant for the Militia with power to choose his Corporal there," and to be in command of such armed forces as were then there. He was a yeoman, as the deed says, which indicates that he considered himself a gentleman farmer. He was also constable.

Three days after this deed was signed, on September 19, 1686, Andros got these eastern settlements, as well as that of New York, again under his rule. By a royal order the "ffort and County of Pemaquid in Regard of its distance from New Yorke, was detached and placed under 'Sir Edmond Andross,' Captaine generall and governour in chiefe of the territories and dominions of New England."

Before this action was taken, the inhabitants of the Sheepscott and Dartmouth plantations had grown restless under the strict military regulations of Dongan and had petitioned for relief. The Monhegan inhabitants did not sign this petition although they must have felt the ill effects of the restrictions.

Naturally the regulation in regard to entering and clearing only at Pemaquid worked a hardship on these outlying communities. Smuggling was the result. It was impossible for any government to rigidly enforce such regulations when opportunity for evasion was so easy of accomplishment as in hundred-harbored Maine.

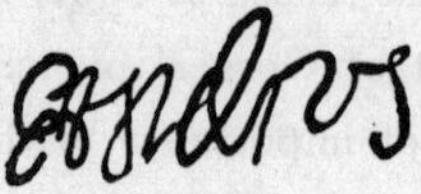

While Andros was pursuing this course of tyrannical rule over the puritanical and turbulent colonists, a revolution had taken place in England. King James II was forced to abdicate and flee for his life to France from the fury of William of Orange and the Protestants. William immediately seized the throne and reigned with Mary from 1688 until 1702. James II had been a violent, unpopular monarch. He had been converted to Catholicism, and had made an alliance with Louis XIV of France, which was extremely distasteful to the mass of the English people.

When the news of the overthrow of James II reached Boston the Americans, remembering Andros' past abuses, took this golden opportunity to seize Andros and fifty of his most active supporters, and throw them into the Boston gaol. They were finally sent to England in 1689 to stand trial.

King James found his revenge in stirring up the French to war on the English. The French and Canadians being anxious to regain their former possessions and also to obtain additional territory to the south, in the disputed region, now set out in earnest to lay waste the English settlements.

For years the Jesuit priests had been inciting the Indians, of the Penobscot and St. Lawrence regions, to hatred of the English under cover of religion. The Indians needed little urging to pillage, burn, destroy, and murder heretics. The results were that another and more terrible Indian war started.

One cause of the intense hatred of the French toward the English in this region is to be found in the unwise action of Deputy John Palmer, of Pemaquid, some time before, or during Dongan's administration in 1687. He seized a ship with a cargo of wine belonging to the French Baron Castine, in the debatable territory, and as this cargo consisted of seventy pipes of Malaga, one of brandy, two of oil, and seventeen barrels of fruit, the Baron was mightily angered and raised considerable trouble, so much in fact that it became an international question. But the ship and cargo were finally restored to Castine.

There is a letter which tells something about this incident, and also of a visit made to Monhegan by Castine:

". . . that there was a report amongst the fishermen ye

St. Casteen was come to Penopscott wth a friggott to build a fort there, and y^t Monsieur Villbonne (who was sent last yeare to Coronell Dungon about the ship y^t was seazd at Penopscott) wth the Judge of Port Royall, but I rather thinke an Ingineer, for I am informd he came from France this yeare in the same friggott y^t was att Port Royall last yeare when I was there. They came in the ketch wch was at Monhegonne wch is six leagues from Penaquid, where they arrived the 17 instant. . . .[115]

"Capt. Francis Nicholson to Mr. Povey, Boston, Aug. 31, 1688."

The Baron Castine was given another cause of complaint, this time by Andros. Early in the Spring of 1688 the Governor, with a number of attendants, started on a tour to the eastern parts of his territory. In the course of his journey he arrived at Biguyduce, the residence of Castine, and dropped anchor in front of his house. When Castine found out that Andros was on board, he became suspicious and fled with his family to the woods. Andros landed and with some of his attendants pillaged the Baron's house, but respected an altar that they found there. Andros was also a Catholic. They loaded the plunder on board the ship and left word that all would be restored if Castine would promise "to come under obedience to the (British) king."[116]

[115] *London Documents, of the New York Colonial Manuscripts,* 1688.

[116] Hutch Coll., p. 562.

With France and England at war, undoubtedly Castine, who had made an alliance with the Indians by a marriage with an Indian princess, and who had a family of half-breed children later, took this opportune moment for revenge. The determined Frenchmen with the help of the "frigott," sent the Indians to attack the fort at Pemaquid, this occurred on August 5, 1689, and to destroy the flourishing settlement of Monhegan, the stronghold of the fishing fleets, which did not take place until October.

John Dollen's (Darling) daughter Grace was married to Dennis Higimen (Hegeman, Hegman) of Pemaquid and was captured and carried captive to Canada, along with her husband, during this raid. Her history there is interesting to us as she was probably born and raised on Monhegan.

"She, testifying in Boston on May 31, 1695, Bomazeen being present, recites her tale of woe.[117]

"She said there were two or three hundred attacking Indians, but no Frenchmen. Her master was 'one Eskeon, a Canadian Indian.' Taken to the Penobscots she was 'very hardly treated by them, both in respect of Provisions & Cloathing, having nothing but a torn blanket to cover me during the winter Season and often-times cruelly beaten,' and continuing: 'After I had been with the Indians three years, they carried me to Quebeck and sold me for Forty Crowns unto the French there, who treated

[117] Coleman, *New England Captives Carried to Canada, 1677-1760*, vol. 2, p. 167.

me well, gave me my liberty and I had the King's allowance of Provisions and also a Room provided for me and liberty to work for my selfe. I continued there two years and a halfe,' during which time a child was born."

This would indicate that her husband was taken captive with her, for the records of the baptism of their child, Joseph, contains his signature:

"The 5th March 1693 was baptized by me François Dupré curé de Québec, Joseph born yesterday, son of denys egman Englishman and gres dalain, his wife, the god-father was le sieur François pachiot, the god-mother Louise douaire wife of sieur Pino who have signed.

Denys Hegman Louise Douaire
pachoss
François Dupré."

"With three Frenchmen she was taken to St. Johns where she stayed three weeks; thence to Port Royal where she spent the winter, and in May, 1695, she was brought to Boston by Abraham Boudroit of Port Royal."

The destruction of Monhegan must have taken place about the middle of October. There is no story of this burning and ravishment of the Island available. Monhegan naturally, even with the one hundred men that were probably here, with the experienced Sergeant Dollen as leader, could not stand up against the Indians backed by a "frigott," and assisted by the French. All the inhabitants must have escaped or there would have been some records left. It would not have been easy to surprise the

Island, as approach would have been observed far enough in advance for the inhabitants to have fled in their boats, which manned by such able seamen as were these Monheganites would have made their escape.

That this destruction took place the following item from Cadillac's *Memoirs* plainly shows:

"Three leagues to seaward there is an island called Meniguen. There were about twenty families employed in fishing around this island, but our Indians have made them abandon it."[118]

This place was undoubtedly destroyed by fire, for the remains of charred wood was often found in the old cellars afterwards, and Sullivan in his *History of Maine* tells of John Dollen's return to his burnt cabin at Monhegan.

A few notations from the records of the towns of Massachusetts of this year give us light on the date of the destruction, and also the fact that some of the inhabitants escaped as undoubtedly they all did. Charlestown was the port reached by:

"John Palmer and his son John. From Monhegan, Oct. 21, 1689."

"Peter King, with wife and three children. Oct. 21, 1689. From Monhegan."[119]

There is also a record of a John Palmer, Sr., and John Palmer, Jr., as owners of land in Boston.[120] John Dollen

[118] M. La Mothe Cadillac's *Memoirs*, vol. 6, p. 283.

[119] *Selectmen's Record, Charlestown, Mass.*, 1689.

[120] *Book of Possessions of Boston.*

and family went to Boston, as we infer from deeds, signed by him later, give that place as residence.

There is immeasurable pathos in the destruction of this island, the oldest English settlement in New England, which had remained peaceful during all the changes of ownership, wars, and troubles of the times, and had sheltered the fishing boats for more than two hundred years. It may well have been that many of the inhabitants were descendants of the men sent over by Gorges, when he planted the Island in 1608 or 1609. All the labor that they had so joyously expended on building their homes, and clearing out fields, bounded by the stone fences that wander even today through the deep woods, was wasted. These fences and the cellars are all that remain of their heroic efforts to establish themselves in the new and free world. An occasional spoon, button, bricks, pieces of broken clay pipes and old bits of iron from an old cellar, and an axe head unearthed from under a foot or more of sod, are mute evidences of their occupations and habits. There is one spoon, seemingly Dutch and of bronze, which was deposited by Mr. Sabine a long time ago in the Maine Historical Society, at Portland. It may have belonged to the Woorring family, as the name is Dutch, and the family was here in 1674.

CHAPTER XVIII

THE records of the occupation of the Island, after the departure of the colonists, and the destruction of the houses by the Indians, are very meager. That the fishing fraternity still came, after a time, we know, and also that residents on the mainland came in the summer to fish and dry their catch is probable. The long seige of five more Indian wars prevented the owners from coming back.

During the reign of William and Mary a charter effected the complete consolidation of Maine with Massachusetts. By this charter all white pine trees of two feet in diameter, at one foot from the ground, were reserved under a penalty, for masts for the Royal Navy. This happened about 1691, and so Monhegan was now utilized for a rendezvous for the American forces engaged in the French and English War. We find that in 1696 Major Church used Monhegan as an outpost:

"Major Church made his way to Monhegin, which being not far from Penobscot, where the main body of our enemy's living was. Being in great hopes to come up with Army of French and Indians before they had scattered and gone past Penobscot, or Mount Desert, which is the chief place of their departure from each other after such acting.

"Having a fair wind, made the best of their way into

Monhegin and there lay all day fitting their boats and other necessities to embark in the night at Mussleneck (a point in Monhegan Island) with their boats. Lying

MAJOR CHURCH

there all day to keep undiscovered from the enemy. At night the Major ordered the vessels all to come to sail, and carry the forces over the bay near Penobscot. But having little wind, he ordered all the soldiers to embark on board the boats with eight days provision, and sent the vessels back to Monhegan, that they might not be discovered by the enemy; giving them orders, when and where they should come to him."

With things in such an unsettled condition, freebooters, privateers, buccaneers and that type of gentry ranged the seas, and piracy was the order of the day. Undoubtedly Monhegan was often a port-of-call for this fraternity. It is a legend of the Island that the notorious Captain Kidd buried some of his booty here, and there are also legends of treasures buried by other miscreants. They are not substantiated by records, however.

King William died in 1702 and Anne Stuart came to the throne of England. This united Scotland with England again, but as she declared war on Louis XIV, of France, and Spain, conditions rapidly became terrible. Another French and Indian War commenced in 1702, and raged for eleven years, until a peace with France and England was concluded in 1713. But the Indians continued their depredations for several years longer. By this treaty France gave up Nova Scotia and Newfoundland and although they were supposed to have given up Louisburg, on the island of Cape Breton, which was so strong that it was regarded as another Gibraltar, it continued to be a menace to the country directly to the south.

Anne died in 1714 and the miserable George I and his descendants came to the throne. The history of Massachusetts under this family of monarchs is too well known to readers for any more mention of it to be made here.

In 1715 Samuel Annis and his wife Naomi, according to a deposition made by Naomi about 1768, states that:

". . . she with her husband Samuel Annis went to live at a place called round Pond . . . and there they continued three Years and then moved off for fear of the Indians to Monhegan Island. And moved off and on for the Space of one Year. And after two Years more the(y) moved off to Monhegan Island. Again for about a month for fear of Said Indians, and then returned to said Round Pond."[121]

Mary Cowell, in a deposition of August 19, 1768, says:

". . . about Fifty years ago (1718) living at a place called Muscongus at the Eastward about seven or eight years . . . that in the summer season, this Deponent with William Hilton, Richard Pierce, Samuel Annis and their Familys used to go over to Monhegan Island for fear of the Indians and return in the Fall . . . that said Samuel Martin used to make fish likewise on Monhegan island on account of the Indians."

The Reverend Richard Baxter of Medfield, Mass., a missionary to the Indians, made a note in his Journal, August 13, 1721:

". . . we arrived at Mun-Hegan where we found several

[121] *Trans. Coll. Soc. Mass.*, vol. 6, pp. 33-36.

fishermen, and some Families yt were removed from Muscongus for fear of ye Indians."

Mr. Baxter, the next day, took several of these families with him to the fort on Georges River.[122]

The fishermen were obliged to keep constant watch for the Indians, for, by 1724, they had grown so confident that they conceived the idea of preying on fishing boats. They first made one or two captures, as one schooner or another put in at some inlet along the coast. So successful were they that they made up a fleet of fifty canoes, intending to go to Monhegan, but probably on account of adverse weather they went to the Fox Islands instead, where there was a considerable number of fishing vessels, which they seized.

To guard against these attacks on so important an industry as the fishing was, the American forces established an outpost on Monhegan. There are two letters of Thomas Westbrook, dated 1724, to his Commander-in-Chief, Lt.-Governor Drummer, that show that this was a fact, and as they also yield some local color they are here given:

"May it Please your Hon^{r}:

"My letter of the 21st of last month wch gave an Acc^{t} that Lieu^{t} Bean was not returned. This accompanys him with a Coppy of his Journal by which your Hon^{r} will be Inform'd of his march. Cap^{tn} Harmon went East among the Islands the 26th of last month in quest of the

[122] *New Eng. Hist. & Gen. Reg.*, vol. 21, p. 55.

Enemy with fifty five men. I am this day sending the Sloop down to Monheigen Island where he is to repair to in case he want anything. I sent Lieu^{t} Lane from this place the 30th of last month with twenty four men a Scout on the backs of the Towns from this place to Berwick only to stop at Saco Falls to guard the People to get down their Log.

"Wee have not heard anything of the Indians for some time past so that its generally thought they are getting into a body. Mine of 20th of last month gave an Acc^{t} that I had dismist Forty Two of the new Imprest men, there is dismist thirteen Since.

"I have p'mitted Lieu^{t} Bean to wait on your Hon^{r} by which he is in hopes he may get his back wages for his being Pilott, whome I have Improv'd as such according to your Hon^{r} orders from the date of his Warrent to this day. I am y' Hon^{re} Dutiful and humb^{t} Servt

"Thos Westbrook

"The number of men as near as I can get the acc^{t} that are now in the Service is about Four hundred.

"Falmouth, June 2^{d}, 1724"

"May it please your Honor

"Captain Harmon is return'd from his Cruise, whom I mett at Monheigon, he informs me your Honour has given him leave to go to Boston to make up his Roll. The Enclosed is a Coppy of his Journal by which your Honour will be Inform'd of his Cruise.

"I am your Honours dutiful and Hum^{bl} Servt

"Tho[s] Westbrook.

"Sagadahock, June 5, 1724."[123]

The fishermen, however, were coming back every season, and we find that William "Vaughn" extensively engaged in the commerce in fish at that time, established quarters here in 1730. While this latter fact has not been verified, it has been so stated in one authority. He may have been a descendant of the William Vengham, who was here in a former period. It has also been stated that Vaughan's papers and records were probably burned, as were so many of that time.

England, Spain and France were again at war by 1744, and the French and Indians renewed their attacks on the settlers and fishing folk and established themselves at Louisberg, and William Vaughan assisted in the historic capture of that fort. But again a Treaty of Peace was signed by England and France in 1748, at Aix-la-Chapelle.

The Pemaquid Proprietor, as the heirs of Davidson, of Boston, styled themselves, with Shem Drowne as agent, held all this territory during this period. This included the many islands that belonged to it, of which Monhegan was one.

Deacon Shem Drowne, probably thinking that this peace would last, bought Monhegan from the heirs and assigns of Davidson, in 1749, for £10, 13 shillings. Shem

[123] *Me. Hist. Soc. Coll.*, ser. 1, vol. 10. Trask, "Letters of Thomas Westbrook, 1722-1726."

Drowne was the skillful artisan who made the gilt-bronze figure of an Indian, with drawn bow and arrow, which perched upon the top of the cupola of Province House of Boston. His handiwork, too, the grasshopper vane of Faneuil Hall, which was in imitation of one on the London Exchange. Shem Drowne also bought the interest that the Pemaquid Proprietors (of which company of

BOSTON, AUG. 27, 1763. THIS MAY CERTIFY THAT THE ABOVE VOTES IS A TRUE COPY. FROM THE PEMAQUID PROPRIETOR'S BOOK OF RECORDS. AND THAT THE SEAL THEREUNTO AFFIXED IS THE COMMON SEAL OF THE SAID PROPRIETY. PR. THOMAS DROWNE, PROP. CLERK

merchants he was a prominent member) had in all the islands belonging to them when he bought Monhegan. "For Eighteen hundred Pounds, Old Tenor Including his Twenty Five Ninetyths. To be paid in Twelve months without Interest."

But even yet the French and Indian wars were not

over, for again England and France went to war in 1756, but this time the fight was fought to a finish, and with the fall of Quebec and the Peace of 1763, the danger from Indian ravages was over. The settlers were no longer prevented from going about their peaceful pursuits on Monhegan.

In the meantime Deacon Drowne had transferred Monhegan to his son Thomas on November 15, 1758, for a few shillings. This deed included, ". . . the small Islands adjacent, the Menahnahs."

Shem Drowne

That the fishermen chanced capture by fishing at Monhegan during this year is evident from the following item, which is found in a list of captives sent, in response to the Proclamation of the Governor:

"Samuel Day, Rufus Stacy — Minhegin Is. a fishing, July 6, 1758."[124]

"In the beginning of July, at the eastward, one Chapels, that lived on Cape Newagen Island, at the mouth of the Scheepscot River, being a-fishing, with two men and a boy, in a schooner, — off Mohegan Island, so called, and near George's River, — were killed, and their schooner burnt."[125]

[124] *New Eng. Hist. and Gen. Reg.*, XIV, p. 273.

[125] Nile's *"History of the Indian and French Wars." Mass. Hist. Soc. Coll.*, 4th ser., vol. 5, p. 461.

Thomas Drowne, after holding Monhegan for some years, sold it on February 6, 1770, to a family of Bickfords; Benjamin Bickford, of Beverly, Mass., yeoman; George Bickford, and Edmund Bickford, shoreman, who may have been sons or grandsons of the George Bickford living here in 1674; and Ebenezer Bickford, merchant, all of Salem, Mass., for £160. By this deed the Island was estimated as containing 400 acres, with a dwelling house and barn. Manana, called Monehauk, was also included in the deed, and was estimated as containing 40 acres. These owners were well equipped to handle not only the fishing industry, but to till the soil, keep a store, and raise live stock.

The Bickfords did not keep the Island for long, however, selling it in 1777 to Henry Trefethren, a cabinet-maker of Kittery, for £300, but owing to the death of George Bickford the conveyance was not made until 1790. Henry Trefethren, who was a Revolutionary soldier, died in 1807, and was buried on Monhegan. His property had previously been divided between his heirs: his son, Henry, and his two daughters, Mary, wife of Josiah Starling, and Sarah, wife of Thomas Horn. Those who are interested in tracing this family will have little trouble, as full information is given by Mr. Charles Francis Jenney in his erudite "Fortunate Island of Monhegan," and also in J. W. Porter's "Island of Monhegan," *Bangor Hist. Mag.*, vol. III, Feb., 1888, p. 141.

As far as this research has extended nothing of unusual importance occurred at Monhegan during the Revolutionary War, although the search has not been wide, for this period. The few references that were found are in two letters:

"Letter from John Waite to the Hon. J. Powell

"Falmouth 31^{s} Aug., 1777.

"Sir — I received from Council a packet of Letters on Public Service with directions from the Honb^{le} Mr. Sewall to forward them to Mechias by a special Messenger. I consulted with Several Gentlemen of this Town who were of the opinion that the Cheapest & greatest dispatch would be to send them by Water, upon which I immediately Hired two Men and two mast Boat who set out last Wednesday with said Packet for Mechias but were unhapily taken off Monahegan by the *Rainbow Barge* and Kept a few Hours and then released as being that (thought) by the Enemy to be only on a Fishing Voyage — they having sunk the Letters before they were taken. . . ."[126]

". . . Last evening a fishing Boat arriv'd here the skipper of which informs us that on the same last Wednesday afternoon they saw four large Ships a few Leagues about S. E. off Monhegin & another vessel at so large a distance they could not determine what it was — at the same time they heard a few Cannon which seem'd to be fir'd at the S. W. of them.

"Sam'l Freeman."[127]

[126] *Me. Hist. Soc. Coll.*, vol. 15, p. 186.

[127] *Me. Hist. Soc. Coll. Doc. Hist.*, vol. 17, p. 2.

Taking these two letters together, they suggest that Monhegan's harbor was occupied by British ships. This seems reasonable to suppose, as the British now had to watch the French, and the Canadians, as well as the Americans, and Monhegan would have been a most strategic port for their operations.

The period between the close of the Revolutionary War and the War of 1812 was a time when smuggling and privateering was the accepted thing. While Maine suffered through the loss of seamen, impressed on British ships, still when war was declared against Great Britain it was exceedingly unpopular here. Maritime interests could only see ruin and disaster. Great Britain filled Maine with her men-of-war, and many of the citizens and others began privateering and smuggling and importing contraband goods on their own account, while both governments winked at the violations.

There is an interesting description given by Josiah Starling, grandfather of Mrs. Ella Pierce now living on Monhegan, then a boy, of the fight between the *Enterprise* and the *Boxer* during the War of 1812; which occurred in sight of Monhegan, and which was told in a grocery store in Casco by "Siah," an old man, which I have given in full:

"Siah Starlin, who saw the famous sea fight off Monhegan, between the British brig *Boxer* and the Yankee privateer *Enterprise,* relates how it all took place.

"'I r'member it, 's if 'twaz yisterday. I saw the hull on'

it—'n' 'twaz a big fight. We lived on M'nhiggin 'n them ar days, 'n' 'twixt farmin', 'n' fishin', 'n' the like, managed t' git on with a big fam'ly o younkers. The *Boxer* an' *Rattler* hed bin standin' off 'n' on M'nhiggin, the hull summer, watchin' fer coasters; 'n' a *gret* many hed bin destroyed; 'n' pressin' the sailors inter the British sarvice, a matter consarnin' which I allers hed my own idees; but arter a while the *Rattler* went off, leavin', the *Boxer* cruise'n on her own hook. The day, afore the fight, waz Saturday. We began t' dig the pertaters: 't hed been a dry summer, and the pertaters ripened off arly. Thet arternoon, the coast-ters hove 'n sight. The British gut sight on 'em, 'n' launched her barges; but they didn't 'mount ter nuthin'; fer they'd scursely left the ship afore a 'shavin'-mill' cum aout o' New Harbor 'n' driv' 'em back. Thet's wut they called privateers 'n them days.

"'Ther wuz 'a gret movin' 'bout on the *Boxer,* t' git under sail. A Signal-gun wuz fired fer the men as wuz ashore after game 'n' berries, 'n' sich; a common enuf happenin'. But gittin' under way, she bore t' west'ard 'thout ketchin' either on 'em, an' finally put inter John's Bay. The nex' day noon, 'twaz the fifth o 'September, we went t' the top o' the hill, takin' a spy-glass with us, 'n' there we wuz jined by three officers of the Britisher, the ship's doctor, a leftenant, 'n' a middy, who wuz ashore, gunnin', the day afore, 'n' didn't hear the signal. They wuz gettin' the lay of the'r ship; but the only sail 'n sight, wuz a brig off Seguin, bearin' daown the s'utheast side of M'nhiggin.

"'Wut brig 'z thet?' asked the surgin, o' father.

"'It's the *Enterprise,'* wuz the reply, arter a long look.

"'The surgin' sed t' the leftenant in 'n undertone, — I heerd it all, ef I wuz a boy, — "Ef Cap'n Blyth takes 'er, he's t' hev a fine ship w'en we git hum."'

"'The *Boxer*'d discivered the brig, 'n' under full sail, steerin' 'bout sou-sou-est, bore daown the bay, but tew late, fer the Yankee shot squar' cross 'er bow, hauled upt' the wind, keepin' t' th' s'uth'ard past M'nhiggin in sarch 'f the *Rattler,* w'ile the Britisher gave starn chase. The *Rattler* hed gone.

"'The Yankee hauled in sail 'n' gut reddy for 't fight. The *Boxer* cum up, 'n' poured in a wild bro'dside, w'en the *Enterprise* whirled short on 'er heel, 'n' jest raked the *Boxer* fore 'n' aft. A few minits arter, she passed her starn with a secon' rakin' fire. The *Boxer* wuz completely outsailed. In less then a half-hour, a third rakin' fire wuz sent 'cross the *Boxer's* bows, thet bro't daown the main-topmast 'n' er number o' men who wuz tryin' t' tare her flag from whar it had bin nailed, — 'n' the fight wuz over. The ships wer' side by side, 'n' the smoke hed drifted abut ter sea. 'Twuz jest a good workin' breeze, 'n' the *Enterprise* sailed raond 'n' raond her enemy, no daoubt disabled the fust fire.

"'The officers bo't a boat of father 'n' put off t' th'r own ship, but wuz not allowed y' bo'rd 'er. So they cum back t' the farmhouse for shelter over night.

"'Supper wuz over, 'n' mother 'd cleared the things

away. 'Twuz mos' dark, w'en ther wuz a rap on the door; father went t' see w'at wuz the matter, an' it wuz the officers cum back.

"'Mr. Starlin', we hev no money, but aour guns ar' jest aout on the porch 'n' you may hev 'em 'n' welcome, ef you'll take us in over night.'

"'Gran'mother cum t' th' door an' said, "I hev em, my son!" She'd taken the guns 'n' hidden 'em.' "[128]

Although "Siah" says that it was in the fight between the *Boxer* and the *Enterprise* that the surgeon and his companions were left on Monhegan, Johnston says that this occurrence was in connection with a fight between the *Crown*, a privateer out of Halifax, and the *Increase*, a vessel commanded by Commodore Tucker, a local undertaking out of Boothbay, which happened in the same locality, and in which the Americans under Tucker were victorious, on April 26, 1813.[129]

There is another story connected with the *Boxer* and her actions that gives a good picture of the time, which we are including:

"To Capt. Geo. H. Preble, U. S. Navy,

"Cambridge, Mass.,

"Sept. 9, 1873.

"At the commencement of our war with Great Britain in 1813, the United States had but few if any factories for the manufacture of woolen cloths, and slept under

[128] Sylvester's *Pioneer Settlements of Maine, Casco.*

[129] Johnston, *Bristol, Bremen and Pemaquid,* p. 403.

British blankets; and the soldiers were clad in British cloths and slept under British blankets. It was understood no captures would be made of British goods, owned by citizens of the United States, and many American merchants imported via Halifax and St. John, N. B., their usual stocks of goods. In 1813, I went with others in the

BURROW'S MEDAL

From Drake's *Nooks and Corners of New England Coast*

Swedish brig *Margaretta* to St. John, N. B., and filled her with British goods, intending to take them to Bath, Maine, and enter them regularly, and pay the lawful duties thereon. All we had to fear was American privateers; and we hired Capt. Blythe, of H. B. M. brig *Boxer* to convoy us to the mouth of the Kennebec River, for which service we gave him a Bill of Exchange on London for £100. We sailed in company, and in a thick fog off Quoddy Head, the *Boxer* took us in tow. It was agreed that when we were about to enter the mouth of the river (Kennebec), two or three guns should be fired over us to have the appearance of trying to stop us, and should any idle folks be looking on. Capt. Burrows, in the United States brig *Enterprise*, lay in Portland Harbor, and hearing the guns got under way, and as is well known captured the *Boxer* after a severe engagement in which both Captains were killed. Our bill of exchange we thought, might in some way cause us trouble, and we employed Esquire K. to take 500 specie dollars on board the captured ship and exchange them for the paper, which was found in Capt. Blythe's breeches pocket.

"Charles Tappan."[130]

The Act of Separation of Massachusetts and Maine provided that the public lands within the then District of Maine should be surveyed and divided equally between the Commonwealth of Massachusetts and the State of Maine, each to hold its own share in severalty, and while Maine, of course, must possess the jurisdiction, Massachusetts retained the soil of the part assigned to her, in fee simple, exempt from all kinds of taxes as long as it should remain in her possession; and reserved all the rights to protect her lands from depredations and to punish trespassers upon them, which existed when the separation took place.

[130] *Bangor Hist. Mag.*

MONHEGAN

Monhegan, with a valuation of $1,000, was assigned to Massachusetts on the first division, December 28, 1822.

Monhegan was still considered an important and desirable island, evidently, for it was the first island selected by Massachusetts for her portion. That Massachusetts considered herself owner of the soil is certain, for on July 23, 1823, Trefethren, Starling and Horn paid the Commonwealth of Massachusetts £200 for its interest in Monhegan and Manana.

Monhegan had forty-three inhabitants in 1810 and sixty-eight in 1820, according to Moses Greenleaf's *Survey of the State of Maine*, published in Portland in 1829. The lighthouse was installed in 1824 and the fog signal station on Manana in 1854. These have been improved and changed from time to time since. They add greatly to the importance and interest of Monhegan.

CHAPTER XIX

AROUND 1850 the Inscription on Manana came to the attention of various societies and men interested in the search for Norse runes in Maine. They were trying to prove that the Norse in their voyages passed Maine's shores. The Massachusetts people were sure that Vinland the Good was in their territory as the Société Royale des Antiquaires du Nord, of Copenhagen, in studying the sagas and Icelandic records, placed it within the Massachusetts or Rhode Island territories. Books and monographs were written at a great rate to prove that this was a fact. The Dighton Rock and its Inscriptions seemed to some to establish it there. Schoolcraft, however, states that most of the so-called inscriptions on the Dighton Rock were of Indian origin. When the Dighton Rock went down, the Inscription on Manana was thrown into the discard as well, although Schoolcraft seems to have thought it to have had Norse characteristics, and was certainly not the work of Indians. To him we are indebted for the publishing of the Inscription.

None of the people interested seem to have studied the maps, or other historical evidence, of the regions, in connection with these inscriptions, and no mention was ever made of the country and river Norumbega, the name which sprawled over all the early maps of this locality.

MONHEGAN

As has been stated in a previous chapter, this name Norumbega is the faint clue which holds the Norse tradition to the shores of Maine. Bega, the city described by Ingram, was undoubtedly situated somewhere near Bangor.

As the Inscription has come in for so much discussion, the articles written by the older men are included in this place.

In 1808 the Reverend Dr. Jenks,[131] of Bath, Me., an oriental scholar, had his attention called to the queer characters on a ledge on Manana by Maj. Joshua Shaw of Bath.

At the meeting of the American Academy of Arts and Sciences in 1851 Dr. Jenks exhibited a copy of the "Inscription on a rock in the small island of Mananas, near the island of Monhegan," and offered the following remarks:

"The great simplicity of the strokes, their resemblance to marks for merely scoring articles, often made in the delivery of bulky merchandise; and the supposition, also, that they might have been the occupation of some idle hour, had led me to undervalue them, and speak of them but slightingly. Since, however, mentioning them the last time, before a meeting of the Antiquarian Society, I have had opportunity of seeing the elaborate report on the subject of the American Indians, made by Mr. Schoolcraft, in which he gives an index of the celebrated Dighton Inscription. This has been dilated on by Prof. Rafn, copi-

[131] *Hayward's Gazetteer,* 1851, p. 64.

ously. But Mr. Schoolcraft has apparently proved that there are two inscriptions of widely differing origin — that the one may be Runic, and certainly not Indian, since nothing of an alphabetical character appears in any of their paintings; and that the other is decidedly Indian, as testified by Chingwauk, his examiner and expert in Indian picture narratives.

"On reading this opinion, which appeared to me more reasonable than any I had seen, I reviewed my transcript, and comparing it with various Runic alphabets of various ages exhibited by Hickes in his Thesaurus, and by Prof. Rafn and his coadjutors in their various publications, I found that all the characters or combinations of them, except one, were decidedly Runic, or could be so supposed on good ground; and even that one might possibly be accounted for in some of the known variations of the alphabet or its contractions. The last two of the characters are precisely similar to the last two of the Runic motto chosen by the Royal Society of Northern Antiquaries, and printed on some of their volumes.

"In the Dighton Inscription not more than six or seven characters are claimed as Runic; or even Phoenician, Punic or foreign.

"Here are eighteen at least. They are on the side of a ledge of rock, near the middle of the little island, or as Williamson writes it, Mennannah, which is separated from Monhegan Island only by a narrow strait that forms the harbor of the latter.

"The island of Monhegan is only about three leagues from the nearest shore of the continent, and was very early and long frequented after the English began to colonize the country. It consists of 1000 acres, and has nearly 100 inhabitants; the little island containing the inscription consists of but 2 acres.

"The characters themselves were reported to me as being about six inches in length, and from a quarter to half inch deep. On the top of the rock, also are three excavations, made about one foot apart, triangularly, from 2 to 3 inches in diameter and about one inch deep, as if for receiving a tripod."[132]

In *Hayward's Gazatteer* the statement is made:

". . . that the rock is either granite or gneiss. Is it probable that any one would 'score a reckoning' in such a hard substance?"

This article also calls attention to a spring near.

Dr. A. C. Hamlin, of Bangor, to whom we are indebted for the drawing of the inscription, published in Schoolcraft's works, says in a discussion of the Inscription on Manana:

"I will not venture to say that the characters are Runic, but will only suggest the possibility of their being made by some illiterate Scandinavian, whose knowledge of the Runic form was very imperfect. If they are recognized as Runic, they belong to that compound, complex, and pointed class which renders an interpretation extremely diffi-

[132] Am. Acad. of Arts & Sciences, vol. 2, *Proceedings,* May 23, 1851.

cult. The pointed class, however, belongs to those times in which the Northmen are supposed to have visited our shores — the 10th-11th, and 12th centuries. The earlier the rune the more simple it was in form and the more easy of translation, but the modifications and corruptions of later periods have confused and changed the character in a great degree.

"Mr. Williamson, the historian of the state, says that about two centuries ago, the early settlers when clearing the lands on the banks of the river found remains of chimneys and mouldering ruins, over which grew an ancient forest. These may have been the remains of Leifsbudir — the relics of seven centuries.

"If this scrawl was not made by Leif or his companions, it may have been made by Karlsfne, during the voyage made in search of the lost Thorhall, when sailing north from Vineland he came to lands which presented in every view noble and majestic forests; or, perhaps, by Thorwald in his expedition in the direction of Maine in the year 1004.

"For three centuries the Icelandic accounts maintain that the Northmen visited our coasts and it is not improbable that some of the bold Vikings were attracted to this island whose advanced position and lofty heights presented the earliest view of land to the mariner approaching the coast of Maine, and here they rudely attempted to commemorate their discovery, or inscribe hurriedly to the memory of a departed comrade.

"I have little doubt that the rock on which the inscription occurs was fissured at first somewhat by nature, and that advantage was perhaps embraced by the Scandinavians. . . ."[133]

Schoolcraft says:

"It is conjectured that Vinland comprised the area at present occupied by the States of Maine and New Hampshire; and the island appears to have been that of Monhegan, contiguous to the coast of Maine. An ancient inscription, traced in letters resembling pointed Runic characters has been found on the face of a rock on that island, from a plaster cast of which the drawing on a reduced scale has been made. This inscription has not been critically examined, but appears to belong to an early, and perhaps to the eccentric age of the art. Dr. Hamblin, expressed the opinion that the Wineland river, which the Scandinavians entered, was the Kennebec, the mouth of which is distant about two leagues from the island of Monhegan. In confirmation of this opinion he stated, that when the first settlements were made on the Kennebec, about 1657, the settlers, as they cut down and cleared off the trees found the remains of chimneys and mouldering ruins, which had been overgrown by the forest.

"This new theory of the location of Vinland will not have to encounter the nautical and astronomical objections, which have been urged against the geographical

[133] Hamlin, in *Am. Assoc. for Ad. of Science,* vol. 10 (1856), p. 214.

position previously assigned to it in Massachusetts and Rhode Island, by the learned Association at Copenhagen; a location which is further, by several days sail toward the south and south-west, than the Sagas indicate. It also avoids the mal-interpretations of the figures and devices on the Dighton Rocks, which are not of Scandinavian origin, or of any alphabetical value whatever.

"These are in the ordinary style of the Indian kekeewin, or mnemonic pictographs."[134]

Rufus King Sewall has the following account of an expedition of the Maine Historical Society to Manana:

"One object of the historical excursion of the U. S. Steamer, *McCulloch,* Sept. 1872, under the administration of the Hon. E. E. Bourne, President of the Maine Historical Society, was an intelligent observation of the localities of sundry rock-written appearances, reported on the islands off the coast of Maine, in and about N. L. 44°, Lincoln County.

"For three generations rumor had floated traditions thereof on shore; and a little girl, a native resident of Damariscove, told Dr. Leonard Woods, of the committee of Historical Research in that expedition, that she knew there were Chinese letters on the rocks of that island, and undertook to lead the way thereto.

"In Maine our coast environments have ever been remarkable features to all ocean travelers, especially the

[134] Schoolcraft, H. R., *History of the Indian Tribes of the U. S.*, vol. 6, of the Ser. 1857.

islands, highlands and mountains showing in N. L. 43° and 44°."[135]

No decision seems to have been reached by the visitors, as a committee, which shows, as might have been expected, that a more experienced guide was essential, for one visitor, C. W. Thornton, the author of *Ancient Pemaquid*, who later became unfriendly with the Maine historians, has the following to say of the Inscription:

"In the autumn of 1872 the Maine Historical Society visited Monhegan Island for the purpose, among other things, of making an examination of the so-called Runic inscription alleged to be seen there. I was present on that occasion by invitation of the Society.

"This runic inscription is not on Monhegan proper but on an isle close by, called Monanis by the famous Capt. John Smith. The characters forming it were on the vertical surface of a dark-colored rock, perhaps trap dike (I am not a geologist) fitted closely into a hard granite rock. At the bottom of all, or nearly all of these so-called runic characters, there was plainly to be seen a crack in the rock. This circumstance and some others forced me to the belief that these characters were made by the operation of nature and not by any human agency. Mr. Morsae's *mutatis mutandis* applied to the Monanis Rock. C. W. T."[136]

This críticism plainly shows that the visitors on that occasion were looking at some cracks, as there is no evi-

[135] Sewall, R. K., *Ancient Voyages to the Western Continent.*
[136] *Am. Hist. Soc.*, vol. 2, p. 308.

dence of trap rock nor of cracks at the bottom of the characters on the Inscription even today. Of course, like all inscriptions exposed to the weather, and made with crude instruments, it is hard to get a light on it that shows the letters plainly. Rather recently I was shown a drawing made by one of the investigators for a famous university which was evidently made from a different set of cracks, for the letters had cracks running out about a foot or so. It is quite evident that many of the authorities who have been so harsh have never even seen the real alleged Inscription. This is easy to understand as your author made two visits and then finally had to be shown where it was. These mistakes have been made because the so-called authorities have called the Inscription rock a ledge instead of a great boulder.

Daniel Wilson, in his *Prehistoric Man,* speaks of the Inscription:

"One of the latest discoveries of these supposed records of the Northmen was produced before the Ethnological Section at the Albany meeting of the American Association, in 1856, by Dr. A. E. Hamblin, of Bangor, and is described in the printed transactions. . . . Dr. Hamblin suggests that it is the work of some illiterate Scandinavian, whose knowledge of the runic form was very imperfect, and he then proceeds to adduce reasons for assigning Monhegan, the Kennebec River, and Merrymeeting Bay, as the localities of Leif's wintering place in Vinland, instead of the previously assumed Pacasset River and

Mount Hope Bay. Dr. Hamblin, however, duly forwarded a copy of the inscription to Copenhagen;[137] and a version of it appears in the Seance Annuelle du 14 Mai, 1859, bearing a very remote resemblance to the accompanying engraving of it, and looking a great deal like runes than the original can possibly do. The Danish antiquaries on this occasion, however, abandoned the attempt at interpretation, although there is something amusing in the contrast between the New Englander's theory of an illiterate Norseman scrawling incomprehensible runic characters on the rock, and that of the Danish elucidator's assumption that 'The Indians have, without doubt, profited in various ways by their intercourse with the Northmen, to whom they were probably indebted for much knowledge; and it is apparently to their instruction, acquired in this manner, that we owe several of their sculptures on the rocks which are met with in these regions.' The Monhegan inscription, thus bandied about between illiterate Northmen and Indians, is in regular lines about six inches long and runs obliquely across the face of a rock, where the general line of horizontal stratification presented no impediment to its characters being placed in the usual upright position."[138]

One of the last attempts to judge of the authenticity of the Inscription that has reached your author is found in the following report:

[137] The copy was broken in transit to Copenhagen.

[138] Wilson, Daniel, *Prehistoric Man,* p. 98, 1876.

"In the summer of 1885, Mr. G. H. Stone of Portland, Maine, published the results of a careful study of the inscription on Manana, made on the spot. He says:

"'When one first sees the inscription rock, he cannot fail to notice that the appearance is as if a tablet had been prepared upon the surface of the rock, not horizontally but obliquely. There are two parallel furrows about one-half an inch deep, and eight inches apart; and the so-called letters are on this tablet. . . .

"'Examination shows that this apparent tablet is simply the exposed edge of a fine-grained vein, which penetrates the coarser grained rock obliquely. . . . The parallel furrows, which inclose the so-called inscription tablet, are simply furrows of weathering at the sides of the vein.

"'The supposed letters are composed of straight furrows intersecting each other obliquely, so that most of them are some modification of the letters V and X. . . . At the base of the furrows I invariably found a crack in the rock, though sometimes not readily without the aid of a magnifier. There are two systems of these joints,—one nearly vertical, the other nearly at right angles to the sides of the vein. Nearly all the furrows forming the supposed inscription belong to these two systems of joints. . . . Most of the joints are filled with a film of oxide of iron. . . . It is evident that the inscription is a freak of surface erosion. The furrows the result of weathering along the joints.

"'It is singular what a striking resemblance the story

of Monhegan's inscription bears to that of the famous Rock of Runamo, in Sweden, which created quite a commotion among the Scandinavian antiquaries and men of science several years ago. Saxo Grammaticus, a learned antiquary and historian who flourished in the 12th century, relates in his history of Denmark, that King Waldemar I, his contemporary, who was also distinguished for his interest in antiquarian studies, had made an ineffectual attempt to have a supposed inscription copied and deciphered, that was found upon a rocky footpath which runs by the sea shore near the village of Hobby, in the south-eastern part of Sweden. In 1838, the eminent Swedish chemist pronounced all those fissures to be natural forms.' "[139]

Your author, who has recently studied the Inscription on Manana, does not agree with Mr. Stone in his statement about the outlining of the tablet by furrows. No sign of this outlining by furrows was found in former examinations, or are they apparent today although the tablet appears to have been smoothed and prepared for the letters. If this is the action of nature, why are there no other signs of like character on the adjacent rocks and why have the cracks not continued outward? What, also, about its being above a large spring?

Joseph Williamson has this to say:

"Stone inscriptions, like that existing in the north of Europe, have been found along our coast. That on Menanas, a small island near Monhegan.

[139] *Mass. Hist. Soc.*, Jan., 1888.

"It is engraved with a sharp instrument upon the vertical face of a ledge, in a ravine which extends some distance across the island, where glacial action could not operate, to leave as it has done all over the rocks of Maine, unquestioned scratches. It covers a space of about 4 ft. long by 6 inches wide. The characters are composed of straight lines, resembling the Runic letters N. W. L. V. and X.

"It will be remembered that Leif, after sailing two days and nights from Markland or Nova Scotia, reached an island. This may be supposed to have been Monhegan from the following circumstances:—On the horizon, mountains blue with distance were seen. Such the Camden hills appear to the observer at Monhegan.

"'The Island lay east of the main land,' says the account. This is the position of Monhegan. From this island the Northmen entered a neighboring river, through which they were carried into a lake filled with salmon.

"Near by, their houses were erected, and they passed the winter. The river is well represented by the Kennebec, which joins the ocean near Monhegan, and Merrymeeting Bay corresponds to the lake. Near the latter have been found the stone hearths that have been described.

"It does not require much imagination to connect the inscription with the latter, as the work of the Northmen; the one rudely intended to commemorate their discovery, or to mark the resting place of a companion, and the other as ruins of their winter settlement, the relics of seven centuries. The advanced position of Monhegan presents the earliest view of land to an approaching mariner, and it is not improbable that it attracted the attention of the bold Vikings. We find difficulty in reconciling the description of the temperate climate with modern experience. But the cold winters of New England, compared with those of Greenland, to which the Northmen were accustomed, must have resembled the mildness of spring; and besides, the seasons may have changed. Because grapes are not now indigenous to our soil, we cannot say that they may not have been so in the days of Leif. Early French settlers found grapes in such abundance in Canada that the Island of Orleans, near Quebec, was named by them Isle of Bacchus."[140]

The latest authority to condemn is Edmund Burke Delabarre in *Dighton Rock*, 1928, where he places our Inscription in the chapter entitled Frauds, Rumors and Reports. He says of the Inscription:

"The most famous inscription in Maine, if it be one, is that commonly spoken of as on Monhegan Island, though it is actually on Monanis, close by Monhegan. It has often been described and pictured. Samuel Adams Drake, for example, in his *Pine Tree State*, says it is 'generally attributed to the Northmen or the devil,' although, of course, as in the case of the Dighton Rock, Phoenicians and other strange people have frequently been regarded as its author. Dr. A. E. Hamlin exhibited a cast of it at the Al-

[140] Williamson, Joseph, Maine Hist. Soc., 1888, Feb. 9.

bany meeting of the American Association for the Advancement of Science in 1856, suggestion that it was the work of some illiterate Scandinavian, whose knowledge of the runic form was very imperfect.

"There is nothing in its appearance as pictured to suggest dissent from the opinion expressed by most authorities, including Mallery, Daniel Wilson, De Costa and others, that its markings are only freaks of surface erosion. This opinion appears to have been first expressed on the basis of a careful and trustworthy personal examination by G. H. Stone in *Science* for 1885, and is confirmed, according to Windsor, by later reliable independent investigations."

This latest expression is amusing as Mr. Delabarre does not even know the name of the island on which the Inscription stands. He is repeating from authorities, who as I have said before probably never saw the real Inscription or they would never have said it was in a vein of trap rock and that there were cracks at the bottom of each letter or character. It would take a microscope to find any cracks there, although there is a crack running through the boulder that is readily seen to be a crack and has been so reported. Dighton Rock is quite another matter.

The characters, so far as your author has superficially investigated, more nearly resemble the Phoenician characters given in a table of alphabets rather recently published by the Harvard Press in the *Serâbît Inscriptions on Mount Sinai.* It will take a scholar of greater archaeological experience than any authority so far given to judge of its character, whether cracks or inscription. At least we have the reproduction of it made seventy-five years ago which can be compared with the original, as has been done by your author, and there appears to have been slight change in it with the exception that the last two letters have been partly broken off and a noticeable crack has appeared above the tablet and running down through it. This crack is quite evidently a crack and therefore shows the doubtful examiner the difference between a crack and a chisel mark.

TYPE OF SHIP USED BY GILBERT AND RALEIGH

From New York Public Library Print Room

APPENDIX

Come Here's the Map —

SHAKESPEARE, HENRY IV, pt. I, act II, scene I.

APPENDIX

Date	Map maker or publisher or name of map	Nationality of discoverer or map maker	Discoverer or Voyager	Regional name	Islands that might be Monhegan from the location
1390 to 1400	Zeno	Italian	Zeni brothers	Drogio	Cluster of islands
1500	Cosa	Basque	Columbus Cabot	C. de S. Jorge	Dot
1502	Cantino	Portuguese	Corte-Reals	Cabo-d-licōtu and Baye St. Jhan Baptiste	Small island shown
1521			Fegundes		Small island
1523 1524	Maggiolo	Italian	Verrazano	Prima Vista	Ile de St. Jean
1524 1525	Alonzo de Santa Cruz in *Islario*	Spanish	Gomez	Northern archipelago de Gomez	Cross +
1525	Planisphere of Mantova	Spanish	Gomez		I. St. Jean Estemez
1529	Ribero, Diego	Spanish	Gomez	Archipelago de Esteran Gomez. C. d. muchas yslao.	Il. de Jila Estcaiez
1535	Paris wooden globe	French	Cartier	Aurobegue Norombega Anorobegua	Small island
1539	Crignon			Norumbega	
1540	Agnese, B. Portulan Atlas	Italian		Gulf of Maine shown	Small islands strongly marked
1542	Roze, Jehan	French in English Service	Cabot	Terra Neuve	Illa da Ioam estevez or dot
1544	Cabot, Sebastien	Italian English Spanish		Cabo S. Jorge	S. berto
1546	Desceliers (Agnese map)		Gomez	Arcipel de Estienne Gomez	Cluster of islands
1550 1553	Agnese, B.	Italian			Brissa
1550	Gastaldi in *Ramusio III*	Italian	Cartier	Le Paradis	Louisa

APPENDIX

Date	Map maker or publisher or name of map	Nationality of discoverer or map maker	Discoverer or Voyager	Regional name	Islands that might be Monhegan from the location
1556		French Italian	Verrazano	Auorobaga (Cape dem Uchaaf ilhas)	Brisa
1566	Zalterius of Bologna	Italian		Norumbega	Cluster of islands
1569 1587	Mercator			Norombega	Claudia
1570	Ortelius (world map) Nordenskiod's Facsimile map			Norobega	Claudia
1570		French	Cousin, Jehan	Cabo S. Jorge	S. berto
1580	Dee, John	English		Norombega	Cross +
1582	Lok, Michael	English			Claudia Eredonda
1587	Map in Peter Martyr's *De Orbe Novo*, dedicated to Richard Hakluyt.			Baccalloas is located in Labrador with "English 1496."	
1610	Unknown. Found in Spanish archives at Simancas.	English	Unknown. Probably Pring, Weymouth and others.		Ile St. George
1612 1613	Champlain	French	Champlain	Noranberga Noremberga	Le Nef La Tortue
1614	Smith, John	English	Smith	New England	Barty Iles
1636	Feca, Lucini. *Dell Arcano del Mare,* pub. by Dudley in 1646, 1648.	Italian		Norambega S. Giorgo.	Mapahigon
1652 1663	Heylyn, P.			Norumbega L. 43′ 40″	
1663	De Laet	French		Norumbega	La Nef
1664	Moxon, Joseph	English			Manhiggan

INDEX

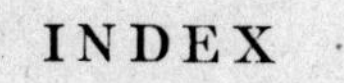

INDEX

INDEX

INDEX

INDEX

INDEX

INDEX

INDEX

INDEX